GW01376077

VISIT ESPRIT.COM

COOL**CITIES**
SAN FRAN CISCO

BERLIN · LONDON · NEW YORK · PARIS · MUNICH · HAMBURG
ROME · MILAN · VIENNA · FRANKFURT · AMSTERDAM · SHANGHAI
BARCELONA · LOS ANGELES · SAN FRANCISCO

Explore the coolest places in COOL**CITIES**, curated by local movers and shakers. Brilliant photos, concise texts, innovative interface design.

teNeues

Available on the App Store

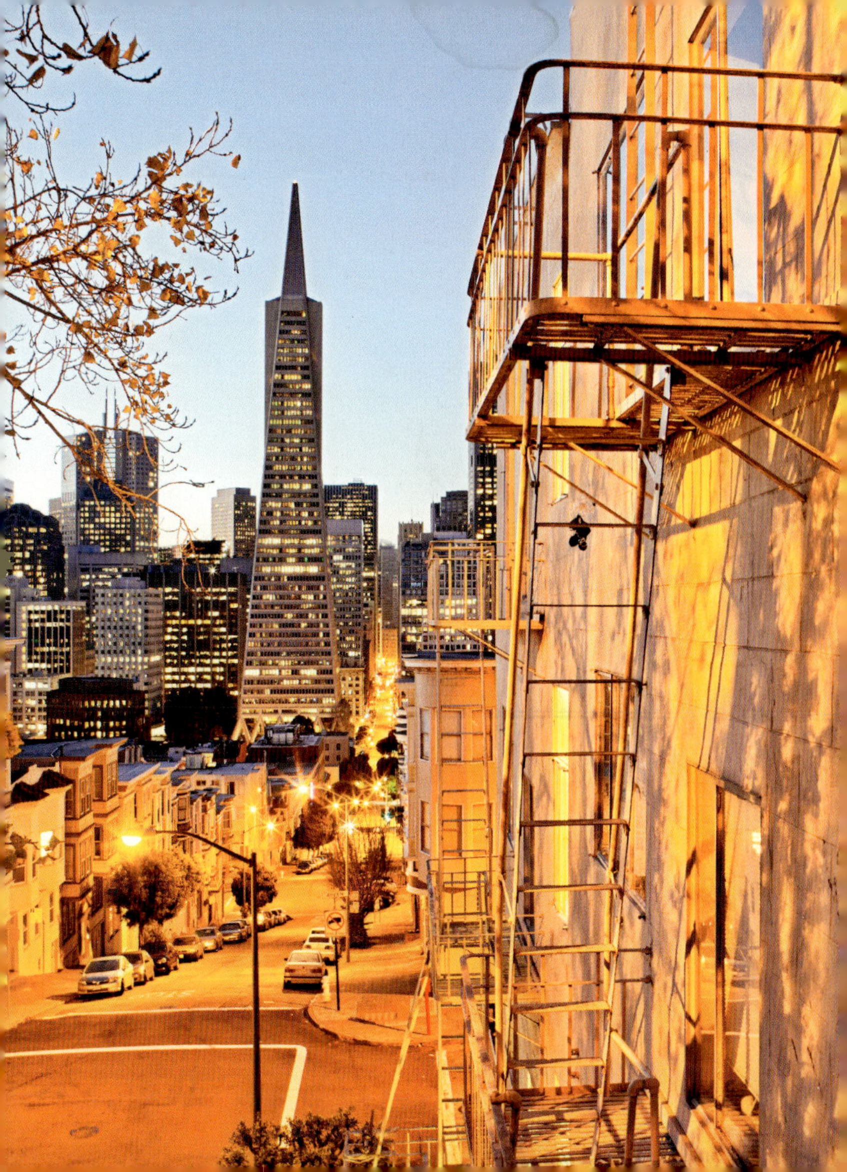

06 INTRO

HOTELS

10 ADAGIO
12 CLIFT
14 FOUR SEASONS HOTEL SAN FRANCISCO
16 PHOENIX HOTEL
18 TAJ CAMPTON PLACE
20 HOTEL DES ARTS
24 HOTEL VITALE
26 ARGONAUT
28 HARBOR COURT HOTEL
32 THE HUNTINGTON HOTEL
34 HOTEL PALOMAR
36 THE MOSSER

RESTAURANTS + CAFÉS

40 ABSINTHE
42 FARALLON
44 FIFTH FLOOR
46 GITANE
48 ZUNI
50 GARY DANKO
52 BAR JULES
54 SUPPENKÜCHE
56 GREENS RESTAURANT
58 SWAN OYSTER DEPOT
60 CAFFE TRIESTE
62 OUTERLANDS
64 AZIZA
66 AQ
68 BAR AGRICOLE
70 SKOOL
72 SOMA STREAT FOOD PARK
74 ANDALU
76 CRAFTSMAN AND WOLVES
78 DELFINA
80 FLOUR + WATER
82 FOREIGN CINEMA
86 LIMON
90 LOCANDA
92 SLOW CLUB
94 NOPA
96 STATE BIRD PROVISIONS

PRICE CATEGORY

$ = BUDGET $$ = AFFORDABLE $$$ = MODERATE $$$$ = LUXURY

COOL CONTENT

SHOPS

- 100 SUI GENERIS
- 102 UNIONMADE
- 104 CARROTS
- 106 AMOEBA MUSIC
- 108 DISH
- 110 INTERNATIONAL ORANGE
- 112 OMNIVORE BOOKS ON FOOD
- 114 CITY LIGHTS
- 118 PAUL'S HAT WORKS
- 120 871 FINE ARTS
- 122 THE VOYAGER SHOP

CLUBS, LOUNGES +BARS
- 126 BLACKBIRD
- 128 LOCAL EDITION
- 130 BOTTOM OF THE HILL
- 134 PUBLIC WORKS
- 136 ZEITGEIST

HIGHLIGHTS

- 140 THE CASTRO THEATRE
- 142 ASIAN ART MUSEUM
- 144 SAN FRANCISCO MAIN LIBRARY
- 146 FERRY BUILDING MARKETPLACE
- 148 PIER 1
- 150 CALIFORNIA ACADEMY OF SCIENCES
- 152 DE YOUNG MUSEUM
- 156 BAKER BEACH
- 158 YERBA BUENA GARDENS
- 160 GREAT AMERICAN MUSIC HALL
- 162 AREA 2881 GALLERY
- 164 CLARION ALLEY
- 168 F.S.C. BARBER
- 170 PHOTOBOOTH
- 174 TWIN PEAKS

EXTRAS

- 176 DISTRICTS
- 177 MAP LOCATOR
- 178 MAP
- 180 CITY INFO
- 185 CREDITS

INTRO

THIS IS THE LEFT COAST—AMERICA'S MOST LIBERAL CITY—AND THAT IDENTITY DRIVES IT TO THE FOREFRONT OF PROGRESSIVE CULTURE. THIS IS THE HEART OF CALIFORNIA CUISINE, WITH ITS LOCAL, ORGANIC INGREDIENTS, SEASONED BY THE ASIAN, MEDITERRANEAN, AND LATIN FLAVORS OF THE CITY'S BIGGEST IMMIGRANT GROUPS. THIS IS THE CENTER OF GREEN ARCHITECTURE AND INCLUSIVE, SOCIALLY-CONSCIOUS CITY PLANNING. THIS IS THE NUCLEUS OF RADICAL ART, POETRY, AND MUSIC, AND THE MECCA OF GAY AND LESBIAN LIFESTYLE AND CULTURE. THE PEOPLE—PAINTERS, GEEKS, VISIONARIES, SURFERS—ARE YOUNG AND TALENTED, TECH-SAVVY AND UNPRETENTIOUS, INFORMAL AND INFORMED. LIKE THOSE WHO SOUGHT PEACE AND LOVE IN 1967, AND THOSE WHO BUILT THE DOT-COM WORLD IN 1997, THEY HAVE COME HERE TO BE A PART OF THE MOVEMENT. THIS IS SAN FRANCISCO: PHYSICALLY AND FIGURATIVELY THE LEADING EDGE OF THE NATION.

SAN FRANCISCO LIEGT LINKS AUSSEN – UND ZWAR NICHT NUR GEOGRAFISCH: ES GILT AUCH ALS DIE LIBERALSTE STADT DER USA. DESHALB IST SAN FRANCISCO IN SACHEN GEGENWARTSKULTUR IMMER GANZ VORNE DABEI. HIER SCHLÄGT DAS HERZ DER KALIFORNISCHEN KÜCHE, MIT IHREN ZUTATEN AUS REGIONALEM BIOANBAU UND DEN KULINARISCHEN EINFLÜSSEN DER GRÖSSTEN IMMIGRANTENGRUPPEN DER STADT: ASIATISCH, MEDITERRAN UND LATEINAMERIKANISCH. HIER BEFINDET SICH DAS ZENTRUM GRÜNER ARCHITEKTUR UND EINGLIEDERNDER, SOZIAL BEWUSSTER STADTPLANUNG. HIER LIEGT DER KNOTENPUNKT RADIKALER KUNST, POESIE UND MUSIK, UND AUCH DAS MEKKA DER HOMOSEXUELLEN UND LESBISCHEN SZENE. DIE LEUTE IN DER STADT – MALER, NERDS, VISIONÄRE UND SURFER – SIND JUNG UND TALENTIERT, TECHNISCH VERSIERT UND UNKOMPLIZIERT, LOCKER UND GUT INFORMIERT. SIE LEBEN HIER, UM TRENDS MITZUGESTALTEN, UM DAZUZUGEHÖREN. GENAU WIE SCHON DIEJENIGEN, DIE IN DEN 60ERN HERKAMEN, UM FRIEDEN UND LIEBE ZU FINDEN, ODER DIEJENIGEN, DIE IN DEN 90ERN DIE DOTCOM-WELT ERSCHAFFEN HABEN. DAS ALLES IST SAN FRANCISCO: GEOGRAFISCH UND KULTURELL DER VORREITER DER NATION.

HOTELS

COOL
SAN FRANCISCO

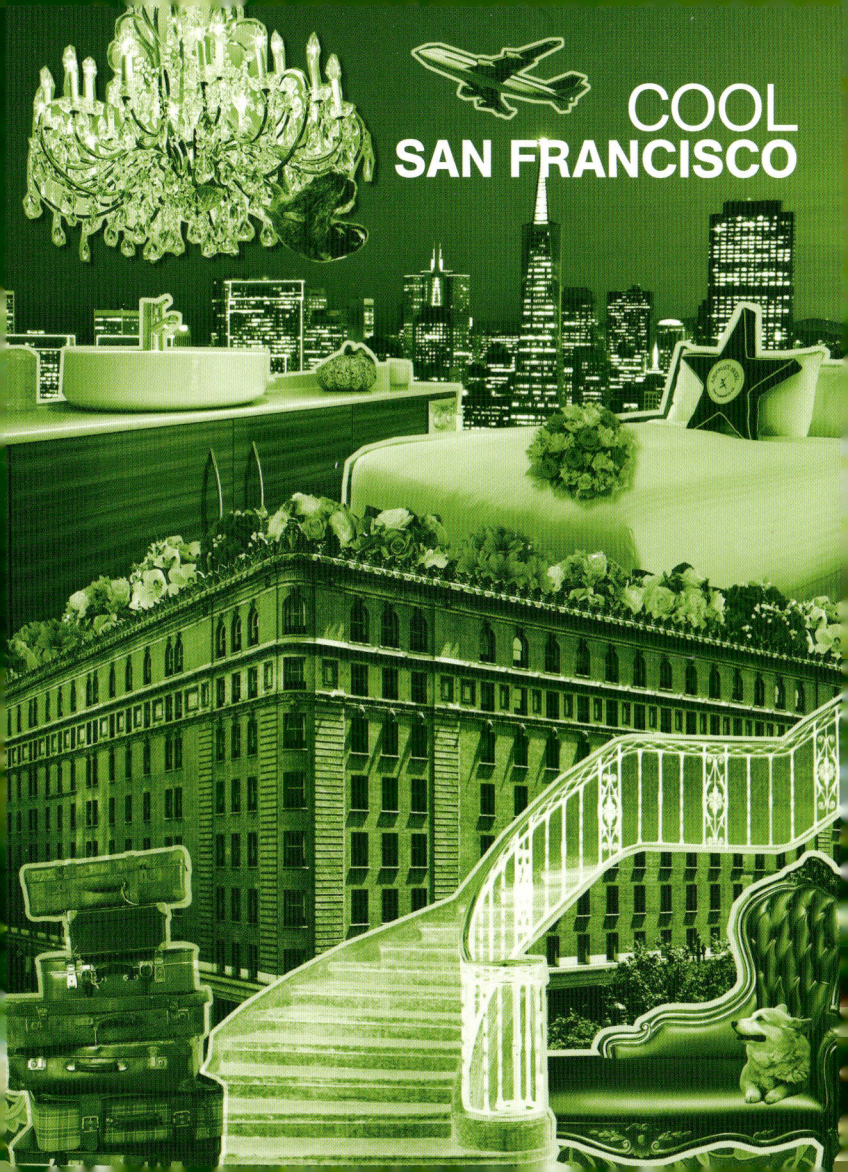

HOTELS

ADAGIO

550 Geary Street // Downtown
Tel.: +1 415 775 5000
www.hoteladagiosf.com

BART, J, K, L, M, N, S, T to Powell
Bus 38 to Geary / Taylor

Prices: $$$

Adagio is a hotel for fans of the theater, located right in the middle of the theater district and featuring a Spanish colonial revival façade. The 171 spacious rooms—all offering a view over the city—are styled in natural shades. The difference to many other hotels in this category is brought about by the small, but fine extras: free daily newspaper, complimentary coffee in the morning, and the regular evening tea in the lobby, inviting guests to get to know each other.

Das Adagio ist ein Hotel für Theaterfreunde, direkt im Theaterviertel von San Francisco, mit einer beeindruckenden Fassade im spanischen Kolonialstil. Alle 171 Zimmer bieten einen Blick über die Stadt, sind geräumig und in Naturtönen eingerichtet. Den Unterschied zu manch anderem Hotel dieser Kategorie machen die kleinen, aber feinen Extras: gratis Tageszeitung, morgens kostenloser Kaffee und der all-abendliche Tee-Empfang in der Lobby, bei dem sich die Gäste kennenlernen können.

MAP N° 1

HOTELS

The neighborhood feels like Broadway with its irresistible mixture of restaurants, shops, and large theaters. And right in the center: the Cliff Hotel. Philippe Starck renovated the 100-year-old luxury hotel, bridging the gap between Art Deco and the straight lines of the 21st century, and setting accents with classic designs by artists like Eames or Dalí. In the evening, long lines of the city's young and wild are vying for a stool at the bar in the legendary Redwood Room.

CLIFT

495 Geary Street // Downtown
Tel.: +1 415 775 4700
www.clifthotel.com

BART, J, K, L, M, N, S, T to Powell
Bus 38 to Geary / Taylor

Prices: $$

MAP N° 2

Die Umgebung erinnert an den Broadway in New York mit dieser unwiderstehlichen Mischung von Restaurants, Shops und großen Musicaltheatern. Mittendrin, das glamouröse Clift Hotel. Philippe Starck hat bei der Neugestaltung des 100-jährigen Luxushotels Art déco mit den geraden Linien des 21. Jahrhunderts verknüpft, Design-Klassiker von Eames bis Dalí setzen Akzente. Abends stehen die Jungen Wilden der Stadt Schlange, um an der legendären Bar des Redwood Room einen Hocker zu ergattern.

HOTELS

FOUR SEASONS HOTEL SAN FRANCISCO

757 Market Street // Downtown
Tel.: +1 415 633 3000
www.fourseasons.com

BART, J, K, L, M, N, S, T to Powell
F to Market / Kearny
Bus 5, 71, 71L to Market / 4th

Prices: $$$$

MAP N° 3

Opened in 2001, the Four Seasons Hotel San Francisco is a child of the hotel boom that kicked off the beginning of the new millennium. The hotel encompasses twelve floors of a 42-story skyscraper in the heart of the Yerba Buena district, just a few steps from Union Square and the Museum of Modern Art. The entire interior is an ode to contemporary elegance, but the highlight is the view: The 277 rooms have floor-to-ceiling windows that frame a fantastic prospect of San Francisco.

2001 eröffnet, ist das Four Seasons Hotel San Francisco ein Kind des Hotelbooms zu Beginn des neuen Millenniums. Das Hotel umfasst zwölf Etagen eines 42-stöckigen Wolkenkratzers im Herzen von Yerba Buena, nur wenige Schritte vom Union Square und dem Museum of Modern Art entfernt. Das gesamte Interieur wirkt unaufdringlich elegant, denn der eigentliche Star ist der Ausblick: Von den bodentiefen Fenstern der 277 Zimmer eröffnet sich eine atemberaubende Sicht über die Stadt.

HOTELS

PHOENIX HOTEL

601 Eddy Street // Downtown
Tel.: +1 415 776 1380
www.thephoenixhotel.com

BART to Civic Center / UN Plaza
F to 9th / Market
Bus 19, 31 to Eddy / Larkin

Prices: $$

MAP N° 4

David Bowie, Moby, Pearl Jam, Franz Ferdinand and Interpol—they've all slept in these beds. Anthony Kiedis, lead vocalist of the Red Hot Chili Peppers, claims it is "sexually, intellectually, and culturally the most stimulating hotel in San Francisco." The architecture brings to mind a clichéd motel of the 1970s, pool and eye-popping sculptures in the courtyard included. Looking for luxury and elegance? Don't go there. But if you are looking for a fun and relaxing stay, you've come to the right place.

17

David Bowie, Moby, Pearl Jam, Franz Ferdinand und Interpol, sie alle lagen schon in diesen Betten. Für Anthony Kiedis, den Sänger der Red Hot Chili Peppers, ist es „das sexuell, intellektuell und kulturell stimulierendste Hotel San Franciscos". Die Architektur erinnert an kalifornische Motel-Klischees der 70er Jahre, mit Pool und poppigen Skulpturen im Innenhof. Fehl am Platze ist, wer auf Eleganz und Luxus steht. Alle, die Entspannung und Spaß haben wollen, sind genau richtig.

HOTELS

TAJ CAMPTON PLACE 19

340 Stockton Street // Downtown
Tel.: +1 415 781 5555
www.tajhotels.com

BART, J, K, L, M, N, S, T to Powell
F to 4th / Market
Bus 2, 3, 30, 45, 76X, 91 to Sutter / Stockton

Prices: $$$$

There's neither flash nor gimmickry about Campton Place—simply a sense of quiet luxury and practiced elegance that suffuses this downtown haven. The décor is understated: soft, neutral hues, balanced by sleek hardwood furnishings. The menu is sophisticated: French cuisine with Indian and Maldivian influences. But the true draw is the pampering, personalized service for which the Taj is renowned. The suites (and the rooftop gym) command the best views of Union Square.

Im Campton Place ist nichts grell oder unnötiger Gag. Stiller Luxus und althergebrachte Eleganz durchfluten diese Oase in Downtown. Das Hotel überzeugt mit subtilem Dekor voll sanfter, neutraler Töne, die mit gepflegten Holzmöbeln harmonieren, mit einer anspruchsvollen Speisekarte voll französischer Kochkunst samt Einflüssen aus Indien und den Malediven sowie mit einem persönlichen Verwöhnservice. Die Suites (und das Sportstudio auf dem Dach) bieten die beste Aussicht am Union Square.

MAP N° 5

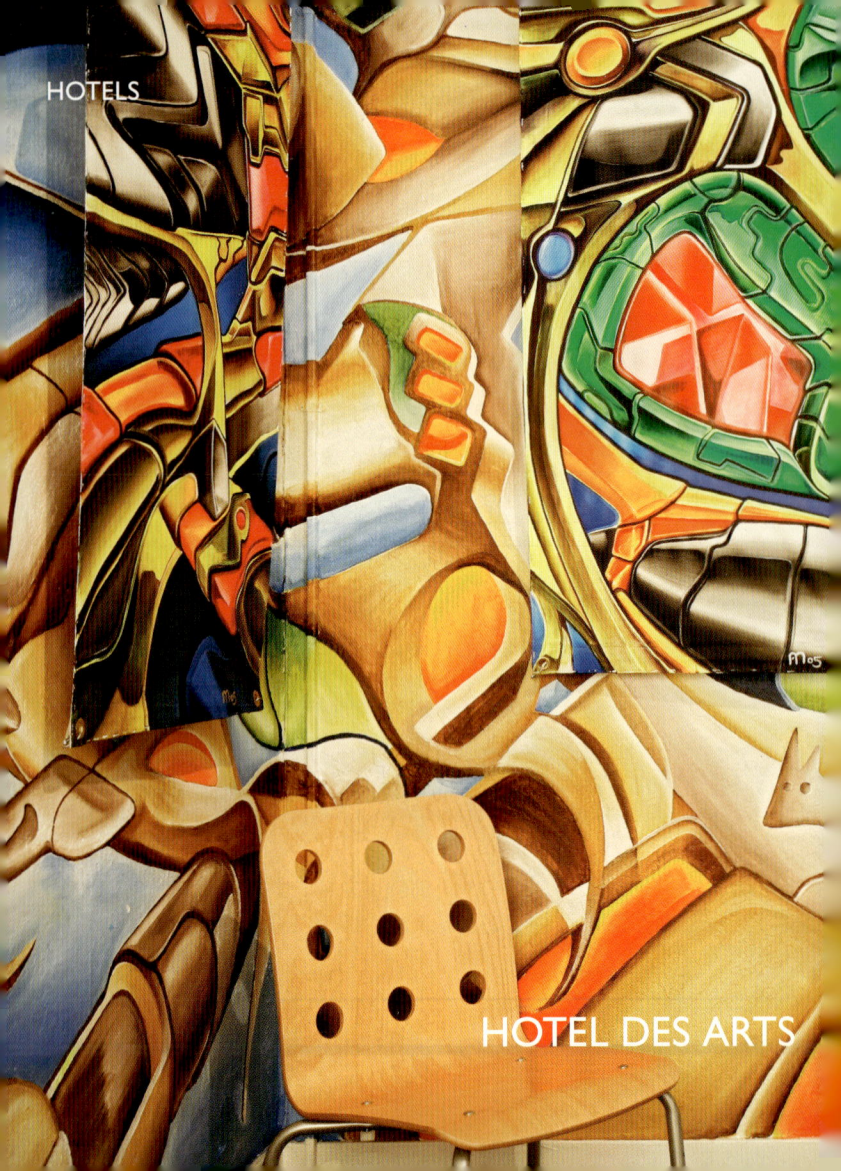

HOTELS

HOTEL DES ARTS

21

HOTELS

"The hotel is a unique art gallery," claims the passionate collector and manager Hero Nakatani. The rooms have been fashioned by emerging local artists. Graffiti virtuoso Sandro Tchikovani, also known as Misk1, is one of them. He has sprayed several walls with his huge word designs. Check out the rooms on the hotel's home page, where they are organized by the artist's name, so you can book based on your artistic preferences. The reasonable price per night includes breakfast.

HOTEL DES ARTS

447 Bush Street // Financial District
Tel.: +1 415 956 3232
www.sfhoteldesarts.com

BART, F, J, K, L, M, N, S, T
to Montgomery
Bus 8AX, 8BX, 8X to Kearny / Bush

Prices: $

MAP N° 6

„Das Hotel ist eine einzige Kunstgalerie", erklärt der leidenschaftliche Sammler und Geschäftsführer Hero Nakatani. Jeder Raum wurde von einem Künstler gestaltet. Graffitisprayer Sandro Tchikovani, Tagname Misk1, ist einer von ihnen und hat mehrere Wände mit seinen großen Formeln besprüht. Sortiert nach Künstler präsentieren sich die Zimmer auf der Homepage, sodass man nach persönlichem Kunstgeschmack buchen kann. Das Frühstück ist im schlanken Übernachtungspreis inklusive.

HOTELS

In a city of mostly Victorian hotels, Vitale boasts a new building by architects Heller Manus, its striking brick-and-glass corner tower gleaming over Ferry Plaza and the Embarcadero. The Zen-modern interior, with its lean settees, wooden paneling, and limestone baths, is elegantly spare and soothing, suited to the hotel's spa-like focus on revitalization. Rooms that look onto the Bay Bridge and Yerba Buena Island are pricey, but the rooftop views are magnificent at sunset—and free.

HOTEL VITALE

8 Mission Street // Financial District
Tel.: +1 415 278 3700
www.hotelvitale.com

BART to Embarcadero
F to Don Chee / Steuart
Bus 6, 14, 14X, 21, 31
to Steuart / Mission

Prices: $$$

MAP N° 7

Vom Architekturbüro Heller Manus konzipiert, thront der Turm aus Glas und Backstein über dem Ferry Plaza und Embarcadero und wirkt so ganz anders als die viktorianischen Hotels der Stadt. Die moderne Inneneinrichtung mit geradlinigen Sofas, holzverkleideten Wänden und Kalksteinbädern passt zur Spa-Atmosphäre des Hauses. Zimmer mit Blick auf die Bay Bridge und Yerba Buena Island sind teuer, aber die Aussicht vom Dach, besonders atemberaubend bei Sonnenuntergang, ist im Preis inbegriffen.

HOTELS

ARGONAUT

495 Jefferson Street
Fisherman's Wharf
Tel.: +1 415 563 0800
www.argonauthotel.com

PH to Hyde / Beach

Prices: $$$

MAP N° 8

Fisherman's Wharf, San Francisco's pepped up fishing port, is full of vibrant life. With its warehouse charm and redbrick appeal, the Argonaut is an island of calm with restaurants, shops, and even bicycle rentals under one roof. The huge lobby is both lounge and museum, where overstuffed sofas sit right next to mementos from San Francisco's nautical history. Right outside the door, street vendors stir their oversized pots and sell Clam Chowder—arguably the best in the city.

In der Fisherman's Wharf, dem aufgemöbelten Fischereihafen, pulsiert das Leben. Das Hotel Argonaut liegt darin wie eine Insel mit Lagerhaus-Charme und Backstein-Chic. Restaurants, Läden, Fahrradverleih – alles ist unter einem Dach vereint. Die riesige Lobby wirkt wie Lounge und Museum zugleich: Deko-Elemente aus der Geschichte der Seefahrt finden sich neben kuscheligen Sofas. Direkt vor der Tür gibt es an Straßenständen, in riesigen Kübeln zubereitet, die beste Clam Chowder der Stadt.

HOTELS

HARBOR COURT
HOTEL

29

HOTELS

HARBOR COURT HOTEL

165 Steuart Street // Fisherman's Wharf
Tel.: +1 415 882 1300
www.harborcourthotel.com

BART to Embarcadero
F to Don Chee / Steuart
Bus 6, 14, 14X, 21, 31 to Steuart / Mission

Prices: $$

Tucked away from the hustle and bustle of the city, but still in a central location: the Harbor Court Hotel. You'll enjoy coming home from a strenuous sightseeing tour: Plop onto your luxurious bed and watch the sun set beyond the Bay Bridge—the unbeatable view of the San Francisco Bay is well worth the additional charge. The cozy lobby offers daily happy hour, and if you are still not tired, catch the historic streetcar at the corner for only $2 and take in some nightlife.

Abseits vom Trubel und doch superzentral liegt das Harbor Court Hotel. Nach einer Sightseeingtour kann man sich hier in luxuriöse Betten fallen lassen und im Liegen hinter der Bay Bridge die Sonne untergehen sehen – den Aufpreis für ein Meerblickzimmer ist dieses Erlebnis allemal wert. Wer nach der Happy Hour vor dem Kamin die gemütliche Lobby noch einmal verlassen möchte, den bringt die historische Straßenbahn an der nächsten Kreuzung für 2 $ ins nächtliche Geschehen.

MAP N° 9

HOTELS

THE HUNTINGTON HOTEL

1075 California Street // Nob Hill
Tel.: +1 415 474 5400
www.huntingtonhotel.com

C to California / Taylor
PH, PM to Powell / California
Bus 1 to Sacramento / Sproule

Prices: $$$

MAP N° 10

If you've made it to the top of Nob Hill, the home of San Francisco's rich and famous, take in the opulent luxury and excellent service at the Huntington Hotel. Entering this distinguished building feels like a journey back in time. Victorian design and antique furniture atop heavy rugs cater to guests who value tradition. The award-winning spa, however, is stunningly modern: Spoil yourself swimming in the pool or sunbathing on the terrace while enjoying breathtaking views.

33

Wer es auf den Nob Hill hoch geschafft hat – seit jeher das Viertel von Wohlstand und Prominenz –, genießt im Huntington Hotel Luxus und ausgezeichneten Service. Diesen ehrwürdigen Bau zu betreten, ist wie eine Zeitreise. Viktorianische Einrichtung, schwere Teppiche mit antiken Möbeln treffen den Geschmack von Gästen, die auf Tradition Wert legen. Atemberaubend modern hingegen ist der preisgekrönte Spabereich mit Pool, Sonnenterrasse und einem hinreißenden Blick über die Stadt.

HOTELS

HOTEL PALOMAR

12 Fourth Street // South of Market (SoMa)
Tel.: +1 415 348 1111
www.hotelpalomar-sf.com

BART, J, K, L, M, N, S, T to Powell
F to 4th / Market

Prices: $$$

Some luxury hotels can feel a little stiff, but not this one. Their lobby greeter sets the tone: His name is Maverick, and he's a Labrador retriever—an affable reminder of the Palomar's famously pet-friendly policies. A stay here is full of clever touches, like guided morning runs through the city, in-room massages, and a daily wine tasting with selections by Fifth Floor Restaurant's Master Sommelier Emily Wines. Borrow a hotel bike to cruise the Embarcadero or visit museum row.

Luxushotels sind oft ein bisschen steif. Dieses nicht. Wenn man in der Lobby von Maverick begrüßt wird, einem Labrador-Retriever, ist das ein klarer Beweis für die (Haustier-)freundliche Art des Hotels. Der besondere Stil zieht sich durch alle Bereiche: Morgens durch die Stadt joggen, Führung inklusive, oder mit dem Hotelfahrrad zum Embarcadero oder ins Museum. Dann eine Massage auf dem Zimmer und abends eine Weinprobe mit Sommelier Emily Wines vom Fifth Floor Restaurant.

MAP N°

HOTELS

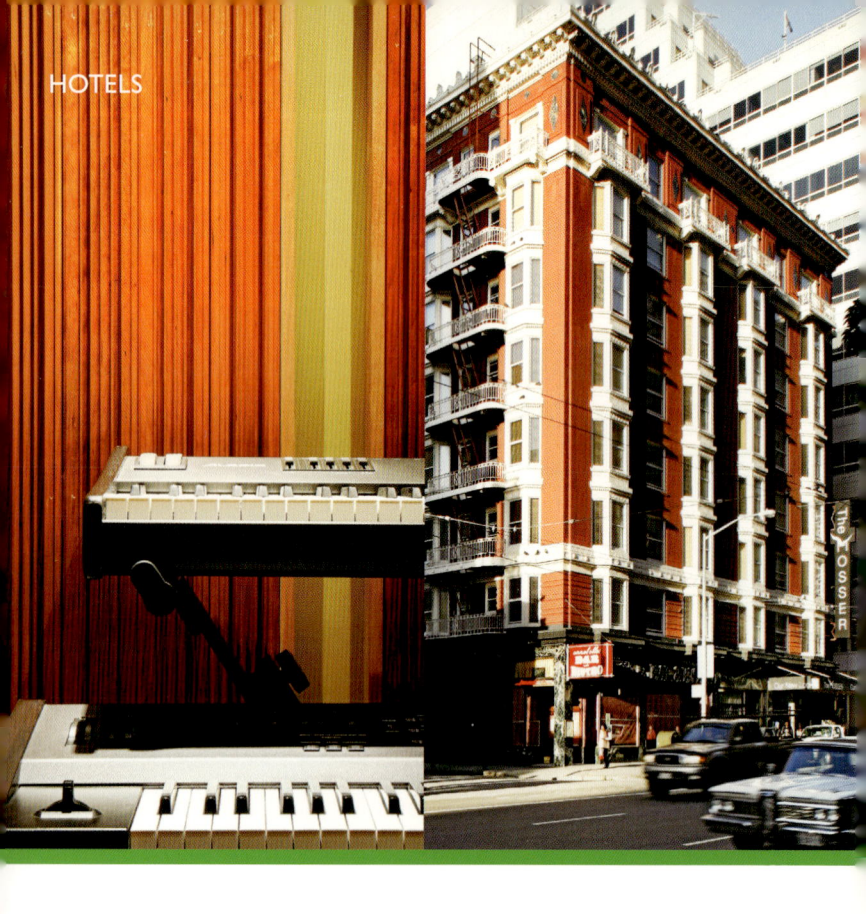

Owned and run by the Mosser family, this somewhat atypical conference hotel sits right outside the Moscone Center, where Apple and others regularly present new products. The hotel is atypical because it also houses Studio Paradiso, a recording studio. And it is atypical because the 166 sometimes small but well designed rooms in the Victorian style building exude a personal and personalized ambience. Recommended for visitors who appreciate affordable quality and style.

THE MOSSER

54 Fourth Street
South of Market (SoMa)
Tel.: +1 415 986 4400
www.themosser.com

BART, J, K, L, M, N, S, T to Powell
F to 4th / Market

Prices: $$

MAP N° 12

Ausgerechnet vor den Toren des Moscone Center – wo u. a. Apple regelmäßig seine Neuigkeiten präsentiert – liegt dieses eher untypische Messehotel. Untypisch, da die Gründerfamilie Mosser mit Studio Paradiso dort auch ein Tonstudio beherbergt. Untypisch auch, weil es mit seinen 166 teils zwar kleinen, aber gut durchdachten Zimmern in dem viktorianischen Gebäude von 1913 viel persönliche Atmosphäre ausstrahlt. Empfehlenswert für Besucher, die preiswerte Qualität und Stil suchen.

RESTAURANTS
+CAFÉS

COOL
SAN FRANCISCO

RESTAURANTS
+CAFÉS

Guys in flip-flops hang at the bar next to distinguished couples in tuxedos and evening gowns. The location of the Absinthe is perfect for a drink before a night at the San Francisco Opera and at the Davies Symphony Hall. And the drinks have what it takes—the barkeepers even wrote a book about that. The lively mood is contagious and makes you think of a Paris bistro. Adam Keough's Francophile cuisine with classics such as onion soup or spicy rabbit meatballs adds to the ambience.

ABSINTHE

398 Hayes Street // Downtown
Tel.: +1 415 551 1590
www.absinthe.com

Tue–Wed 11.30 am to midnight
Thu–Fri 11.30 am to 2 am
Sat 11 am to 2 am
Sun 11 am to 10 pm

F to Market / Gough
Bus 21 to Hayes / Gough

Prices: $$$
Cuisine: American Bistro

MAP N° 13

Hier sitzen Jungs in Flipflops neben Paaren in Smoking und Abendkleid an der Bar. Das Absinthe liegt strategisch günstig für einen Drink vor dem Besuch der San Francisco Opera oder der Davies Symphony Hall. Und die Drinks haben es in sich: Die Barkeeper haben sogar ein Buch darüber geschrieben. Die ausgelassene Stimmung ist ansteckend und erinnert an Pariser Bistros. Klassiker der frankophilen Küche von Adam Keough sind seine Zwiebelsuppe oder die würzigen Kaninchen-Fleischbällchen.

RESTAURANTS +CAFÉS

This historic 1925 Elks Club building would be impressive on its own, but Farallon designer Pat Kuleto has embellished it into an underwater fantasy, complete with jellyfish chandeliers and a 50,000-marble "caviar" staircase. Each room is unique; the Pool Room, with original arched mosaics by 1920s artist Anthony Heinsbergen, is particularly lovely. Naturally, seafood is the specialty here—locals often come just for the happy hour menu of oysters, clams, and truffled fries.

FARALLON

450 Post Street // Downtown
Tel.: +1 415 956 6969
www.farallonrestaurant.com

Mon–Thu 5.30 pm to 9.30 pm
Fri–Sat 5.30 pm to 10 pm
Sun 5 pm to 9.30 pm

BART, F, J, K, L, M, N, S, T
to Montgomery
PH, PM, Bus 2, 3, 76X to Powell / Post

Prices: $$$$
Cuisine: Seafood Grill

MAP N° 14

Das historische Elks-Club-Gebäude aus dem Jahr 1925 imponiert ja schon, doch die Unterwasser-Fantasie von Designer Pat Kuleto brilliert dazu noch mit Lüstern in Quallenform und einer „Kaviartreppe", besetzt mit 50 000 Murmeln. Jeder Raum ist einmalig; im Pool Room finden sich z. B. ausgesprochen schöne Mosaiken von Künstler Anthony Heinsbergen. Natürlich sind Meeresfrüchte hier Programm. Einheimische kommen gern zur Happy Hour und genießen Austern, Muscheln und getrüffelte Pommes.

RESTAURANTS
CAFÉS

FIFTH FLOOR 45

12 4th Street // Downtown
Tel.: +1 415 348 1555
www.fifthfloorrestaurant.com

Mon 5 pm to 10 pm (Bar only)
Tue–Sat 5.30 pm to 10 pm

BART, J, K, L, M, N, S, T to Powell
F to 4th / Market

Prices: $$$
Cuisine: American-International

Each of the three rooms here (lounge, bar, and dining) has a separate menu, and the food, like the décor, is sophisticated, modern, yet not overstated. Chef David Bazirgan incorporates produce from local farmer's markets into Mediterranean-influenced dishes like chicory and chorizo with cabrales and quince. Desserts are often savory: Parmesan ice cream and beet cake, for example. Sommelier Amy Goldberger is renowned for a diverse cellar and excellent, often unusual pairings.

Salon, Bar und Speisesaal haben jeweils eine eigene Speisekarte. Wie das Dekor sind auch die Gerichte anspruchsvoll und modern, wirken aber niemals übertrieben. Chefkoch David Bazirgan kauft zwar lokal, entführt uns aber ans Mittelmeer mit Chicorée und Chorizo, Cabrales-Schimmelkäse und Quitten. Der Nachtisch ist oft pikant: Parmesan-Eis etwa, oder Rübenkuchen. Sommelier Amy Goldberger ist für ihren gut bestückten Weinkeller bekannt, aus dem sie ungewöhnliche Kombinationen zaubert.

MAP N° 15

RESTAURANTS
+CAFÉS

GITANE

6 Claude Lane // Downtown
Tel.: +1 415 788 6686
www.gitanerestaurant.com

Mon–Wed 5.30 pm to 10.30 pm
Thu–Sat 5.30 pm to 11.30 pm

BART, F, J, K, L, M, N, S, T
to Montgomery
F to Market / Kearny
Bus 2, 3, 30, 45, 76X, 91
to Sutter / Kearny

Prices: $$
Cuisine: European

MAP N° 16

Influences of different cultures can be seen in the furnishings of Gitane, just as they can be found in the culture of gypsies after which the restaurant is named. The interior designers combined vintage chandeliers with hand-printed wallpapers, and kitschy tapestries with a solid wooden bar and a cabinet with dusty wine bottles. The menu is an equally wild potpourri: The dishes created by Bridget Batson and Patrick Kelly are a mixture of Spanish, French, and Middle Eastern ingredients.

Genau wie in der Kultur der Zigeuner finden sich auch in der Einrichtung des Gitane die Einflüsse verschiedener Kulturen. Die Innenarchitekten kombinierten Vintage-Leuchter zu handbedruckten Tapeten, kitschige Wandbehänge zu einer soliden Holztheke und einer Vitrine mit angestaubten Weinflaschen. Ein ebenso wildes Potpourri ist die Speisekarte. In den Gerichten von Bridget Batson und Patrick Kelly treffen spanische, französische und orientalische Zutaten aufeinander.

RESTAURANTS +CAFÉS

ZUNI

1658 Market Street // Downtown
Tel.: +1 415 552 2522
www.zunicafe.com

Tue–Thu 11.30 am to 11 pm
Fri–Sat 11.30 am to midnight
Sun 11 am to 11 pm

J, K, L, M, N, S, T to Van Ness
F to Market / Gough

Prices: $$$
Cuisine: American Bistro

MAP N° 17

With its busy coming and going at the long copper bar, Zuni feels like a bistro in Paris or Rome. Reservations are recommended, but the bar and outdoor tables are available to walk-in guests. The heart of the restaurant is the open kitchen with its wood-fired oven, where all meals are prepared in plain view. Inspired by French and Italian cuisine, Zuni has been one of the city's classic culinary establishments since 1979. Be sure to try the roasted chicken with warm bread salad.

49

Das geschäftige Kommen und Gehen an dem langen Kupfertresen erinnert an Bistros in Paris oder Rom. Auch ohne Reservierung sind Gäste an den Tischen im unteren Barbereich immer willkommen. Das Zentrum des zweistöckigen Restaurants ist die nach allen Seiten offene Küche mit ihrem holzbefeuerten Ofen. Hier entstehen die italienisch und französisch inspirierten Gerichte, die das Zuni seit 1979 zu einem Klassiker der Gastro-Szene machen. Ein Muss: das Brathähnchen mit warmem Brotsalat.

RESTAURANTS
+CAFÉS

GARY DANKO 51

800 N Point Street // Fisherman's Wharf
Tel.: +1 415 749 2060
www.garydanko.com

Daily 5 pm to 10 pm

PH, Bus 30, 47 to Hyde / North Point

Prices: $$$$
Cuisine: Californian

After winning a James Beard Award for Best Chef in California, Gary Danko founded this gourmet mecca, which methodically tops critics' lists of San Francisco's finest food. Diners choose several courses from a nightly prix fixe menu that includes delicacies from horseradish-crusted salmon to juniper-flavored venison with chestnuts and cranberries. A small army of expert servers (they know more than most chefs) attends each table. Want a table? Call six weeks in advance.

Mit dem James-Beard-Preis für „Best Chef" in Kalifornien bewaffnet, eröffnete Gary Danko dieses Mekka für Gourmets, das ganz oben auf der Liste der besten Lokale in San Francisco steht. Ein Prix-Fixe-Menü bietet Delikatessen an wie Lachs unter Meerrettichkruste oder mit Wacholder überbackene Wildgerichte mit Kastanien und Preiselbeeren. Ein Bataillon von Kellnern mit mehr Expertise als manch ein Koch kümmert sich um jeden Wunsch der Gäste. Die Warteliste ist ganze sechs Wochen lang!

MAP N° 18

**RESTAURANTS
+ CAFES**

Jessica Boncutter learned how to cook at the River Café in London, a place that has molded many a modern chef—that's where Jamie Oliver was discovered for TV. Her restaurant seats 38, features an open kitchen with a wood oven range, and its own herb garden. The menu, different every day, offers hearty meals such as eggs-up with fennel sausage or lentils in red wine, fine-tuned with a touch of French finesse. The vegetables come straight from sustainable regional eco-farms.

BAR JULES

609 Hayes Street // Hayes Valley
Tel.: +1 415 621 5482
www.barjules.com

Tue–Sat 11.30 am to 2.30 pm
5.30 pm to 10 pm
Sun 11 am to 2.30 pm

F to Market / Guerrero
Bus 21 to Hayes / Laguna

Prices: $$
Cuisine: Californian

MAP N° 19

Kochen gelernt hat Jessica Boncutter im River Café in London, einer wahren Schmiede der modernen Küchenchefs – Jamie Oliver wurde dort fürs Fernsehen entdeckt. Ihr Lokal hat 38 Plätze, eine offene Küche mit Holzofen und einen eigenen Kräutergarten. Auf die täglich wechselnde Karte kommt Herzhaftes wie Spiegeleier mit Fenchelwurst oder in Rotwein geschmorte Linsen, alles mit einem Touch französischer Finesse. Das marktfrische Gemüse lässt Jessica von Ökobauern aus der Region anliefern.

RESTAURANTS
+CAFÉS

SUPPENKÜCHE

525 Laguna Street // Hayes Valley
Tel.: +1 415 252 9289
www.suppenkuche.com

Mon–Sat 5 pm to 10 pm
Sun 10 am to 2.30 pm, 5 pm to 10 pm

F to Market / Laguna
Bus 21 to Hayes / Laguna

Prices: $$
Cuisine: German

Fabrizio Wiest, a brewer's grandson, left Munich for San Francisco to live his very own American Dream. Good thing he took along his sophisticated knowledge of traditional German home cooking. The Suppenküche serves potato fritters with applesauce, herring the way mom made it, or Sauerbraten with red cabbage and homemade German pasta called Spätzle. A selection of solid wines and German beer completes the menu, which is so delicious even a Bavarian innkeeper would be proud.

Fabrizio Wiest, Enkel eines Brauereibesitzers, zog von München nach San Francisco, um seinen amerikanischen Traum zu leben. Traditionelle deutsche Hausmannskost auf höchstem Niveau hat er glücklicherweise aus der Heimat mitgebracht. In seiner Suppenküche gibt es Reibekuchen mit Apfelmus, Heringe nach Hausfrauenart oder Sauerbraten mit Rotkohl und Spätzle. Dazu bietet er kräftige Weine und deutsches Bier an, in einer Auswahl, auf die selbst ein bayerisches Wirtshaus neidisch wäre.

RESTAURANTS
+CAFÉS

GREENS RESTAURANT

Fort Mason, Building A // Marina
Tel.: +1 415 771 6222
www.greensrestaurant.com

Tue–Fri 11.45 am to 2.30 pm,
5.30 pm to 9 pm
Sat 11 am to 2.30 pm, 5.30 pm to 9 pm
Sun 10.30 am to 2 pm, 5.30 pm to 9 pm

Bus 28, 28L to Marina / Laguna

Prices: $$
Cuisine: Vegetarian

MAP N° 21

Founded in 1979 by Zen Buddhists, Greens became the city's most renowned vegetarian kitchen, and for years, the only waiters were shaven-headed devotees. Then and now, fresh ingredients still arrive from the restaurant's organic garden in Marin. The menu changes daily, but longtime Chef Annie Somerville says, "Our food will always be labor-intensive." Enjoy the waterfront location, and request a table by the window to watch the sun set through the cables of Golden Gate Bridge.

Zenbuddhisten eröffneten 1979 die bekannteste vegetarische Küche der Stadt. Jahrelang wurde man hier ausschließlich von kahlgeschorenen Gläubigen bedient. Das Restaurant mit seiner schönen Lage am Wasser bekommt seine frischen Zutaten von einem Biogarten in Marin. Die Speisekarte ist zwar jeden Tag neu, doch eines bleibt: „Unser Essen ist immer aufwendig", verspricht Chefköchin Annie Somerville. Von den Fensterplätzen aus sieht man die Sonne hinter der Golden Gate Bridge untergehen.

RESTAURANTS
+CAFES

SWAN OYSTER DEPOT

1517 Polk Street // Nob Hill
Tel.: +1 415 673 1101

Mon–Sat 10.30 am to 5.30 pm

C, Bus 19 to California / Polk
Bus 1 to Sacramento / Polk

Prices: $$
Cuisine: Seafood

The lines on the street are up to two hours long, yet loyal fans wait patiently to snatch one of the two dozen barstools at the Swan Oyster Depot. Once seated, you'll get all the attention you'll ever need. Men in the white aprons typical of fish barkers remind you of barkeepers that mix their ever-changing dishes like drinks. The clientele comes back again and again. Why? The family-owned and operated business has been serving the freshest fish in the city for over 100 years.

Bis zu zwei Stunden warten die loyalen Fans geduldig auf der Straße, um einen der zwei Dutzend Barhocker an der Theke des Swan Oyster Depot zu ergattern. Sitzt man, bekommt man alle Aufmerksamkeit der Welt. Die Männer in ihren weißen Fischverkäuferschürzen erinnern an Barkeeper, die ihre wechselnden Gerichte wie Cocktails mixen und eine Kundschaft hinterlassen, die immer wiederkommt. Warum? Weil der über 100 Jahre alte Familienbetrieb einfach den frischesten Fisch serviert.

RESTAURANTS
+CAFÉS

This is where Francis Ford Coppola wrote "The Godfather." Makes sense once you've experienced the authentic Italian ambience at the Caffe Trieste. Here, "Papa Gianni" opened his first coffee shop in 1956, and initiated Americans in the art of enjoying espressos and cappuccinos. The 92-year-old host is a man of many talents: On Saturdays he grabs the mic and entertains his guests with semi-classical Italian repertory, accompanied by his family and the clatter of coffee cups.

CAFFE TRIESTE

609 Vallejo Street // North Beach
Tel.: +1 415 982 2605
www.caffetrieste.com

Fri–Sat 6.30 am to 11 pm
Sun–Thu 6.30 am to 10 pm

F to The Embarcadero / Broadway
Bus 8BX, 8X, 41 to Columbus / Broadway
Bus 10, 12, 41 to Broadway / Grant

Prices: $
Cuisine: Café

MAP N° **23**

Hier hat Francis Ford Coppola „Der Pate" geschrieben. Durchaus verständlich, wenn man einmal die authentisch italienische Atmosphäre im Caffe Trieste geatmet hat. 1956 eröffnete „Papa Gianni" sein erstes Kaffeehaus und weihte die Amerikaner in den Genuss von Espresso und Cappuccino ein. Daneben hat der 92-Jährige ein weiteres Talent: Samstags greift er zum Mikrofon und gibt italienische Schlager zum Besten, begleitet von seiner Familienband und klapperndem Kaffeegeschirr.

RESTAURANTS + CAFES

With its driftwood walls, rough tables, and beer served in Mason jars, Outerlands feels like a cozy surfer shack. Fitting, since it sits walking distance from the foggy waves of Ocean Beach, and its menu of thick soups, sourdough bread, and fresh seafood has been nourishing cold, hungry surfers since its inception. People pack in after hiking at Lands End or lounging at Baker Beach, but the homespun gourmet food is worth the wait—especially the Dutch pancakes at Sunday brunch.

63

OUTERLANDS

4001 Judah Street // Outer Sunset
Tel.: +1 415 661 6140
www.outerlandssf.com

Tue–Thu 11 am to 3 pm, 6 pm to 10 pm
Fri 11 am to 3 pm, 5.30 pm to 10 pm
Sat 10 am to 3 pm, 5.30 pm to 10 pm
Sun 10 am to 3 pm

N, Bus 18, NX to Judah / 46th

Prices: $$
Cuisine: Californian

MAP N° **24**

Wände aus Treibholz, grobe Tische und Bier aus Weckgläsern – Outerlands hat das Ambiente eines gemütlichen Surfer-Schuppens. Passt gut, denn nur wenige Schritte weiter brechen die Wellen am Ocean Beach. Suppen, Sauerteigbrot und frische Meeresfrüchte haben schon manch hungrigem Surfer die Seele gewärmt. Die Kundschaft kommt scharenweise von Lands End oder Baker Beach, doch für die einfachen und leckeren Gerichte lohnt sich die Wartezeit, vor allem für die Pfannkuchen zum Brunch.

RESTAURANTS +CAFÉS

AZIZA

5800 Geary Boulevard // Richmond
Tel.: +1 415 752 2222
www.aziza-sf.com

Wed–Mon 5.30 pm to 10.30 pm

Bus 38, 38BX Geary / 22nd

Prices: $$$
Cuisine: Moroccan

MAP N° 25

Chef Mourad Lahlou serves classic Moroccan dishes like eggplant and lamb shank, but with an inventive and modern touch that transcends the traditional. The bar here is as famous as the kitchen, using savory kitchen spices to create superb cocktails like Tarragon-Cardamom Caipirinhas and Rose Water Margaritas. For a memorable night, splurge on the 13-course tasting menu, and prepare to endure three hours of first-class food and drink in Aziza's sexy arabesque interior.

Chefkoch Mourad Lahlou serviert klassische Gerichte aus Marokko wie Aubergine oder Lammkeule, aber mit einem erfinderisch modernen Stil, der die Tradition verfremdet. Die Bar ist so berühmt wie die Küche: Drinks wie Estragon-Kardamom-Caipirinhas und Rosenwasser-Margaritas werden mit feinen Küchengewürzen aufgemischt. Das 13-gängige Probiermenü ist etwas ganz Besonderes: eine drei Stunden lange Schlemmerei ausgezeichneter Gerichte und Getränke in Azizas sexy-arabesker Atmosphäre.

RESTAURANTS +CAFÉS

AQ

1085 Mission Street
South of Market (SoMa)
Tel.: +1 415 341 9000
www.aq-sf.com

Tue–Sat 5.30 pm to 11 pm
Sun 11 am to 2 pm, 5.30 pm to 11 pm

BART to Civic Center / UN Plaza
F, J, K, L, M, N, S, T to Civic Center
F to 7th / Market
Bus 14, 19 to Mission / 7th

Prices: $$$
Cuisine: Californian

MAP N° **26**

The competition among restaurants in San Francisco is so fierce that anyone braving to open a new one better have an exceptional idea. Matt Semmelhack, owner of AQ, came up with his very own winning recipe: "seasonal." Huge seasonal plants and flowers create the ambience of winter, spring, summer, or fall in his lofty red brick wall interior. The menu experiments with the fresh ingredients from local markets, creating delicious Californian dishes with a gentle French touch.

Wer in San Francisco ein Restaurant aufmacht, braucht gute Ideen, um sich gegen die riesige Konkurrenz durchzusetzen. Das Konzept von Matt Semmelhack, Eigentümer des AQ, lautet: „saisonal". So ist der loftige Innenraum mit Backsteinwänden immer mit großen Pflanzen passend zur jeweiligen Jahreszeit dekoriert. Und die Speisekarte experimentiert mit allem, was der Markt frisch hergibt. Die Gerichte sind kalifornisch, die Zubereitungstechniken meisterhaft französisch.

RESTAURANTS
+CAFÉS

BAR AGRICOLE

355 11th Street
South of Market (SoMa)
Tel.: +1 415 355 9400
www.baragricole.com

Sun–Thu 5 pm to 10 pm
Fri–Sat 5 pm to 11 pm

F, J, K, L, M, N, S, T to Van Ness
Bus 9, 47, 90 to 11th / Folsom

Prices: $$

Cuisine: Californian-Mediterranean

MAP N° **27**

The mixture of recycled oak wood, steal, and concrete creates a clear and open space—a loft with cocktail bar and a landscaped patio. The menu follows the overall concept: eco, high quality, and delicious. The evenings belong to boiled eggs with sea urchin or pork pastrami. During the day, the place transforms into a lounge for the start-up companies in the neighborhood. Architect Joshua Aidlin made sure that Bar Agricole is featured in all renowned architectural magazines.

← DOWNTOWN 69

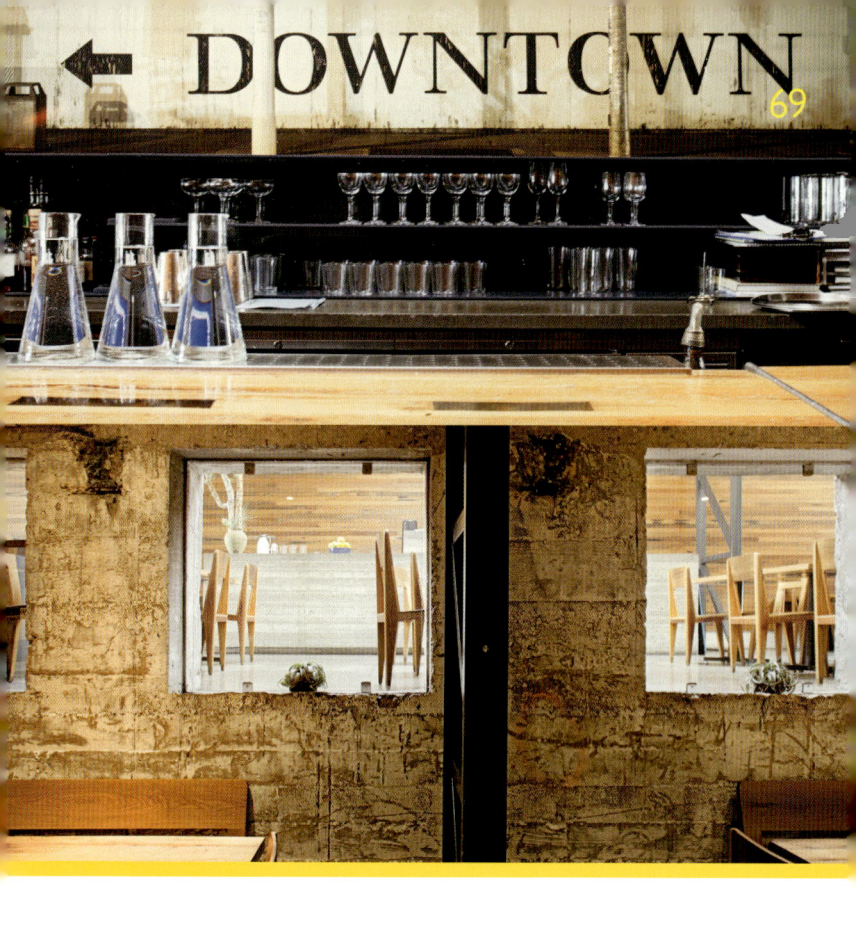

Die Mischung aus recyceltem Eichenholz, Stahl und Beton schafft einen klaren Raum – loftartig, mit Cocktailbar und begrüntem Patio. Die Speisekarte folgt dem Gesamtkonzept: biologisch, hochwertig, delikat. Abends gibt es gekochte Eier mit Seeigel oder Schweinebauch-Pastrami. Tagsüber wird der Ort zur Lounge für Start-ups aus der Nachbarschaft. Dem Architekten Joshua Aidlin ist es zu verdanken, dass die Bar Agricole in den renommiertesten Architekturzeitschriften zu finden ist.

RESTAURANTS & CAFÉS

Chef Toshihiro Nagano values the high nutritional value of seafood. Sardines and mackerel are some of the favorite ingredients of his cuisine, and he prepares them preferably self-smoked. The plain furnishings of the sun soaked room evoke images of a cafeteria, though a first-class and modern cafeteria, no doubt. Skool is the preferred hangout for start-up entrepreneurs, architects, and artists. They come to slurp oysters, eat mussels, or discuss their latest projects.

71

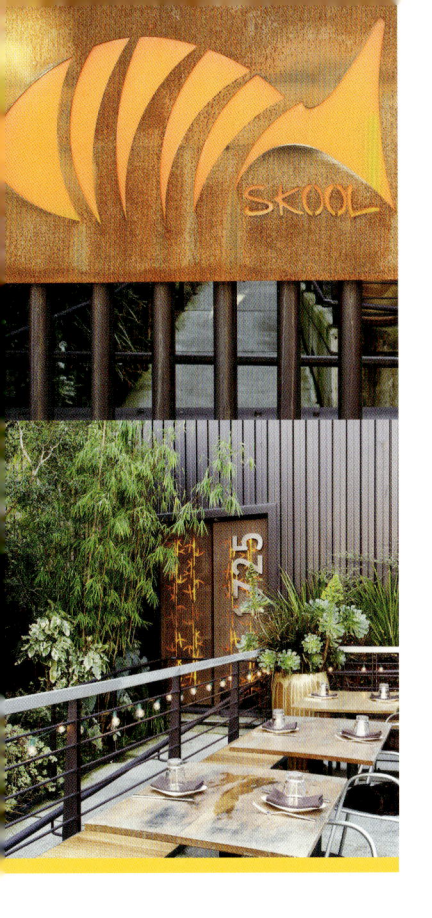

SKOOL

1725 Alameda Street
South of Market (SoMa)
Tel.: +1 415 255 8800
www.skoolsf.com

Mon 11.30 am to 2.30 pm
5 pm to 9 pm
Tue–Fr 11.30 am to 2.30 pm
5 pm to 10 pm
Sat 11.30 am to 3 pm, 5 pm to 10 pm
Sun 11.30 am to 3 pm, 5 pm to 9 pm

Bus 10, 19 to Rhode Island / Alameda

Prices: $$
Cuisine: Japanese

MAP N° **28**

Küchenchef Toshihiro Nagano schätzt den hohen Nährwert von Fisch. Sardinen und Makrelen gehören zu den Lieblingsobjekten seiner Kochkunst und werden von ihm bevorzugt selbst geräuchert zubereitet. Die schlichte Einrichtung des lichtdurchfluteten Raums erinnert fast an eine Kantine, eine moderne und erstklassige, versteht sich. Im Skool treffen sich junge Start-up-Unternehmer, Architekten und Künstler zum Austernschlürfen, Muschelessen oder zum Diskutieren ihrer neuesten Projekte.

RESTAURANTS
+CAFÉS

SOMA STREAT FOOD PARK

428 11th Street
South of Market (SoMa)
www.somastreatfoodpark.com

Mon–Fri 11 am to 3 pm, 5 pm to 9 pm
Sat 11 am to 10 pm
Sun 10 am to 5 pm

Bus 9, 9L, 47 to 11th / Harrison

Prices: $
Cuisine: International

MAP N° **29**

Food trucks are what's in all over California: A kitchen-on-wheels offers a selection of finger food ranging from hot dogs to curry and oysters. An ever-growing fan base follows these food trucks on twitter and facebook throughout the city, hunting down always changing culinary delights. Not up for the chase? Just go to the SoMa StrEAT Food Park. A dozen food trucks rotate in and out for brunch, lunch, and dinner. The covered seating area and the backyard charm are free.

Foodtrucks sind „the new big thing" in Kalifornien. Das ist Küche-auf-Rädern mit Essen-in-die-Hand, egal ob Hot Dog, Curry oder Austern. Eine wachsende Fangemeinde folgt diesen Trucks über Twitter oder Facebook durch die ganze Stadt, süchtig nach immer neuen kulinarischen Kicks. Wer sich's einfach machen will, geht zum SoMa StrEAT Food Park. Dort wechseln sich bis zu einem Dutzend Trucks für Brunch, Lunch und Dinner ab. Überdachten Sitzbereich und Schrebergartencharme gibt's inklusive.

RESTAURANTS
CAFES

The Mission District thrives with the scene of young hipsters who enjoy getting together to laugh, eat, and drink—in a word, to enjoy life to the hilt. The tapas bar Andalu is the perfect expression of this lifestyle. Guests rub shoulders at the small tables and lose themselves in deep conversation while they share appetizer plates full of Californian delicacies like tacos with tuna tartar or ribs braised in Coke. In the sky painted on the ceiling the sun shines even on rainy days.

ANDALU

3198 16th Street // The Mission
Tel.: +1 415 621 2211
www.andalusf.com

Mon–Tue, Sun 5.30 pm to 9.30 pm
Wed–Thu 5.30 pm to 10.30 pm
Fri–Sat 5.30 pm to 1 am

BART to 16th / Mission
F, J to Church / 16th
Bus 22 to 16th / Guerrero

Prices: $$
Cuisine: American

MAP N° 30

Der Stadtteil Mission lebt von einer jungen, hippen Szene, die sich gerne trifft, lacht, isst – kurz, das Leben in vollen Zügen genießt. Die Tapasbar Andalu passt genau zu diesem Lebensgefühl. Hier rücken die Gäste an den kleinen Tischen eng zusammen, sind in ihre Gespräche vertieft und teilen auf vielen Tellerchen kalifornische Leckereien wie Tacos mit Thunfisch-Tartar oder in Coca-Cola geschmorte Rippchen. Der gemalte Himmel an der Decke sorgt selbst an Regentagen für sonnige Laune.

RESTAURANTS
+CAFÉS

A designer boutique for pastries. William Werner, the owner of the patisserie, turns croissants, muffins, and madeleines into fashion objects, and has gained significant exposure by selling his delicacies on markets and in pop-up cafés. The muffin called "The Rebel Within" takes its name from a country western song by Hank Williams III. Pieces of Asiago cheese, green onion, Easton's breakfast sausage, and in the middle a soft-boiled egg—good, hearty fare, and a hit among the die-hard fans.

CRAFTSMAN AND WOLVES

746 Valencia Street // The Mission
Tel.: +1 415 913 7713
www.craftsman-wolves.com

Mon–Fri 7 am to 7 pm
Sat 8 am to 7 pm
Sun 8 am to 5 pm

BART to 16th / Mission
F, J to Church / 18th
Bus 33 to 18th / Valencia

Prices: $$
Cuisine: Café

MAP N° **31**

Eine Designerboutique für Gebäck. Croissants, Muffins und Madeleines werden zu Modeobjekten. William Werner ist Chef der Konditorei, die sich durch den Verkauf auf Märkten und in Pop-up-Cafés einen Namen gemacht hat. Der Muffin „The Rebel Within" ist nach einem Countrysong von Hank Williams III benannt. Stückchen von Asiago-Käse, grüner Zwiebel und Schweinswürstchen, in der Mitte ein gekochtes Ei – klingt ziemlich deftig, ist aber der Hit unter den eingefleischten Fans.

RESTAURANTS +CAFÉS

DELFINA

3621 18th Street // The Mission
Tel.: +1 415 552 4055
www.delfinasf.com

Mon–Thu 5.30 pm to 10 pm
Fri–Sat 5.30 pm to 11 pm
Sun 5 pm to 10 pm

BART to 16th / Mission
F, J to Church / 18th
Bus 33 to 18th / Guerrero

Prices: $$$
Cuisine: Italian

MAP N° 32

Delfina may be small, but it is famous far beyond the borders of California. Everything here is picture perfect: The food that makes it to your table is Italian—Toscan, to be exact—and tastes as delicious as if "la mamma" herself had stirred the pot for hours. The pasta is made fresh from scratch, and the service is charming and attentive. By now Craig and Annie Stoll's gourmet-empire includes four restaurants, all of them cult, but Delfina is where it all began.

Delfina ist klein und berühmt, und das weit über die Grenzen Kaliforniens hinaus. Hier stimmt einfach alles: Was auf den Tisch kommt ist italienisch, genauer gesagt toskanisch, und schmeckt wie von „la mamma" selbst gekocht. Die Nudeln werden frisch zubereitet und der Service ist überaus charmant und aufmerksam. Craig und Annie Stoll haben mit dem Delfina begonnen, sich ihr kleines Gastronomie-Imperium aufzubauen. Inzwischen gehören ihnen vier Restaurants. Alle sind Kult.

RESTAURANTS
+CAFÉS

FLOUR + WATER

2401 Harrison Street // The Mission
Tel.: +1 415 826 7000
www.flourandwater.com

Fri–Sat 5.30 pm to midnight
Sun–Thu 5.30 pm to 11 pm

BART to 16th / Mission
Bus 12 to Folsom / 20th

Prices: $$
Cuisine: Italian

MAP N° 33

As the name implies, this is a simple Italian restaurant: a handful of recycled wood tables, waiters in street clothes, pour-your-own wine. Even the menu is just half a page long. The food, on the other hand, is so inventive and complex that there is usually a line out the door. The handmade pork ravioli are popular, and the pizza, baked for just two minutes in an 800-degree wood oven, is the best in the city. The chef also teaches classes, which include dinner and wine.

Der Name verspricht einen schlichten Italiener: Holztische, Kellner in Straßenkleidung, und den Wein bringt man selbst mit. Die Speisekarte ist nur eine halbe Seite kurz, aber die Mahlzeiten sind so exquisit, dass die Schlange vor der Tür sehr lang ist. Die Ravioli mit Schweinefleisch sind berühmt, und die beste Pizza der Stadt muss nur für kurze zwei Minuten bei 425 Grad in den Holzofen. Wer's lernen will, nimmt Unterricht beim Chefkoch – Dinner und Wein sind inklusive.

RESTAURANTS
+CAFÉS

FOREIGN CINEMA

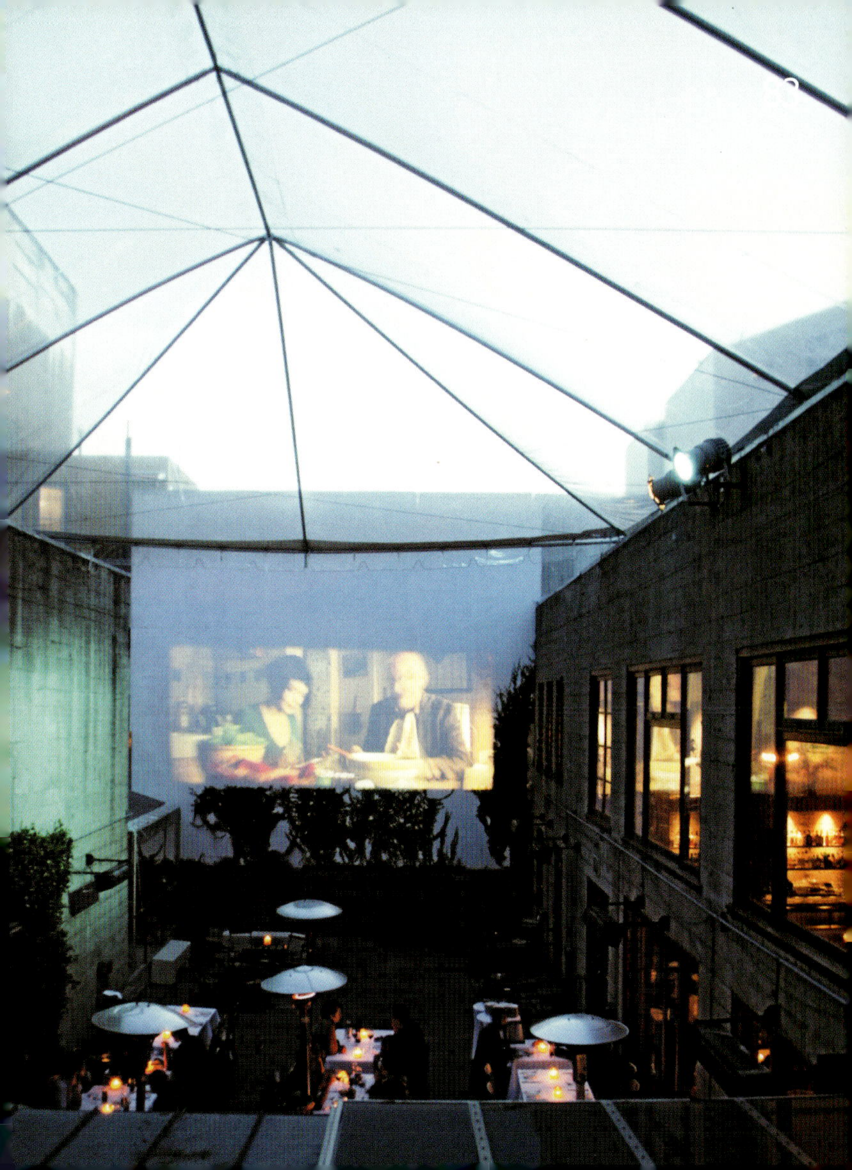

RESTAURANTS +CAFÉS

FOREIGN CINEMA

2534 Mission Street // The Mission
Tel.: +1 415 648 7600
www.foreigncinema.com

Mon–Thu 6 pm to 10 pm
Fri 5.30 pm to 11 pm
Sat 11 am to 3 pm, 5.30 pm to 11 pm
Sun 11 am to 3.30 pm, 5.30 pm to 10 pm

BART to 24th / Mission
Bus 14, 49 to Mission / 21st

Prices: $$$
Cuisine: Californian-Mediterranean

Instead of popcorn and a movie, you'll find a bustling restaurant with a huge courtyard behind the façade of an old movie theater in the city's Mission District, which is known for its nightlife and Latino community. The scene at Foreign Cinema is hip and cool, the food international with dramatic new combinations of ingredients. Once the sun has set, the restaurant honors its name and shows movies from around the world, projecting them on the wall of the building next door.

Mitten im Mission District, der für sein Nachtleben und die Latino-Community bekannt ist, steht ein altes Kino. Doch statt Kinokasse und Leinwand findet sich hinter der Fassade ein meist vollbesetztes Restaurant mit großem Innenhof. Die Szene ist hip und cool, das Essen international mit spannenden Kombinationen der Zutaten. Wenn die Sonne untergegangen ist, macht das Lokal seinem Namen alle Ehre und projiziert an die Wand eines Nachbarhauses Autorenfilme aus aller Welt.

MAP N° 34

RESTAURANTS
+CAFES

LIMON

524 Valencia Street // The Mission
Tel.: +1 415 252 0918
www.limonsf.com

Fri–Sat noon to 11 pm
Sun–Thu noon to 10 pm

BART 16th / Mission
Bus 22 to 16th / Valencia

Prices: $$
Cuisine: Peruvian

Even in an area known for vibrant Latin food, Limon stands out. For one, its modern design with poured concrete, bright walls in tonal lime, and dark wood furnishings is anything but rustic. Two, the busy crowd leans more uptown urbane than thrift-store grunge. Finally, this isn't home-style Mex, it's sophisticated Peruvian: citrus-soaked ceviche, charred octopus, and sirloin saltado. Just don't neglect the classics: crispy, salty rotisserie chicken and cold Cusqueña beer.

Obwohl es in dieser Ecke viele lateinamerikanische Lokale gibt, sticht das Limon heraus. Ganz modern in Gussbeton, die Wände schrill, geht es trotz dunkler Holzmöbel nicht rustikal zu. Die Klientel kauft in Designerboutiquen statt in Secondhandläden, und das Essen ist nicht hausbacken und mexikanisch, sondern anspruchsvoll und peruanisch: Ceviche in Zitrone, gegrillter Tintenfisch und Lendenfilet saltado. Wer's klassisch mag, bestellt ein gebratenes Hühnchen und ein kaltes Cusqueña.

ESPRIT

VISIT ESPRIT.COM

RESTAURANTS
CAFÉS

The menu honors Roman traditions. And to make sure his dishes are as authentic as possible, chef Anthony Strong spent several months in Italy and peeked over the shoulders of local masters. Those who are not familiar with Roman cuisine, be prepared for delicacies like saltimbocca, artichokes Jewish style, lamb, or pancetta, and the ever-present black pepper and Pecorino cheese. The place is always buzzing. Without a reservation you won't be seated until late—if at all.

LOCANDA

557 Valencia Street // The Mission
Tel.: +1 415 863 6800
www.locandasf.com

Mon–Wed 5.30 pm to 10 pm
Thu–Sat 5.30 pm to 11 pm
Sun 5 pm to 10 pm

BART to 16th / Mission
Bus 22 to 16th / Valencia

Prices: $$
Cuisine: Italian

MAP N° **36**

Die Speisekarte folgt römischer Tradition. Um das möglichst authentisch hinzubekommen, war Koch Anthony Strong extra ein paar Monate in Italien und hat dort den Köchen über die Schulter geschaut. Wer die Küche Roms noch nicht kennt, darf sich auf Köstlichkeiten freuen wie Saltimbocca, Artischocken nach Jüdischer Art, Lamm oder Pancetta und immer wieder viel schwarzer Pfeffer und Pecorino-Käse. Der Laden brummt, Tische ohne Reservierung gibt's – wenn überhaupt – erst spät.

RESTAURANTS +CAFÉS

SLOW CLUB

2501 Mariposa Street // The Mission
Tel.: +1 415 241 9390
www.slowclub.com

Mon–Thu 8 am to 2.30 pm
6.30 pm to 10 pm
Fri 8 am to 2.30 pm, 6.30 pm to 11 pm
Sat 10 am to 2.30 pm, 6 pm to 11 pm
Sun 10 am to 2.30 pm

BART 16th / Mission
Bus 9, 33, 90 to Potrero / 17th
Bus 27 to Bryant / Mariposa

Prices: $$
Cuisine: American Bistro

MAP N° **37**

Though Potrero Hill is slightly off the beaten path, Slow Club is always popular—at least, it's perpetually noisy and bustling with trendy, well-heeled diners. Is that due to the focus on local ingredients (the name is a reference to the "slow food" movement)? Is it the appeal of the industrial-yet-intimate décor? The excellent drinks? The hearty brunch menu? Or maybe it's the Prather beef burger, a perennial contender for best burger in the city? Take your pick…and enjoy.

Trotz der Lage etwas abseits auf dem Potrero Hill ist der Slow Club sehr populär. Zumindest ist es dort immer laut und gerammelt voll mit gut betuchten Trendsettern. Liegt das an den ausschließlich lokalen Zutaten? (Der Name bezieht sich auf die Bewegung für bewusstes, regionales Essen.) Oder liegt es an der Anziehungskraft des industriell-intimen Interieurs? Am herzhaften Brunch? Oder am angeblich besten Burger der Stadt, dem Prather Beef Burger? Wer weiß ... deshalb genießen Sie einfach.

RESTAURANTS
+CAFÉS

560 DIVISADERO

nopa

NOPA

560 Divisadero Street
Western Addition
Tel.: +1 415 864 8643
www.nopasf.com

Mon–Fri 5 pm to 1 am
Sat–Sun 11.30 am to 1 am

N to Duboce / Noe
Bus 21, 24 to Hayes / Divisadero

Prices: $$$
Cuisine: Californian-Mediterranean

For a restaurant voted the city's "Best Overall" by locals, Nopa's menu is surprisingly down-to-earth: hearty cannellini and kale soup, incredible pork chops grilled over almond wood, all inspired by Mediterranean peasant food. Owner and chef Laurence Jossel says the local, organic ingredients are key: "I don't need anyone to see how smart I am. I want them to see how brilliant the farmer is." The wine (cellared in an old bank vault) is mostly European, and always excellent.

Einheimische haben Nopas einfache Küche zur besten der Stadt gekürt. Die herzhaften Cannellini, Grünkohlsuppe und über Mandelholz gegrillten Schweinekoteletts schmecken nach mediterraner Bauernküche. Schlüssel zum Erfolg von Besitzer und Koch Laurence Jossel sind die regionalen Zutaten aus Bioanbau: „Ich muss nicht beweisen, wie schlau ich bin. Ich will zeigen, wie brillant der Bauer ist." Der Wein, meist aus Europa und immer exquisit, wird im alten Kellergewölbe einer Bank gelagert.

RESTAURANTS +CAFÉS

The kinetic vibe here is pure dim sum: servers wheel past, hawking bite-size offerings, while diners pluck whatever strikes their fancy. Everyone experiments, including chefs Brioza and Krasinski, who dish up oddities like sauerkraut pancakes that are just as good as favorites like pork ribs over chard, or the namesake crispy quail. Reservations can be difficult, but standing bar side is an excellent option—the best way to watch and appreciate the kitchen's furious alchemy.

STATE BIRD PROVISIONS

1529 Fillmore Street // Western Addition
Tel.: +1 415 795 1272
www.statebirdsf.com

Mon–Thu 5.30 pm to 10 pm
Fri–Sat 5.30 pm to 11 pm

Bus 22, 38, 38L, 92 to Fillmore / Geary

Prices: $$$
Cuisine: American-International

MAP N° **39**

Das Ambiente ist fühlbar Dim Sum: Kellner schieben mundgerechte Häppchen durch das Lokal, und Gäste bedienen sich nach Lust und Laune. Alle sind experimentierfreudig, auch die Köche Brioza und Krasinski, die Kurioses wie Sauerkraut-Pfannkuchen auftischen. Genauso gut sind die Klassiker: Schweinerippchen mit Mangold etwa, oder die namengebende knusprige Wachtel. Wenn es keinen freien Tisch gibt, lohnt es sich auch, von der Bar aus das alchemistische Treiben in der Küche zu beobachten.

SHOPS

COOL
SAN FRANCISCO

SHOPS

SUI GENERIS

2265 Market Street // Castro
Tel.: +1 415 437 2265
www.suigenerisconsignment.com

Mon–Sat 11 am to 7 pm
Sun 11 am to 5 pm

K, L, M, S, T to Castro
F to Market / Noe
Bus 37 to Market / Sanchez

Prices: $$$

MAP N° 40

The name means "one of a kind," and indeed, this consignment boutique stands alone in its assiduously selected assortment of high-end designs. The women's shop has gems like mint McQueen dresses and Chanel jackets at discount prices. Menswear (a few steps down the street) ranges from YSL to Watanabe to Shipley & Halmos, with a nice selection of vintage tees to boot. Attentive service, often from the owners themselves, means accurate fitting, tasteful choices, and little wasted time.

Wie der lateinische Name verspricht, bietet die Secondhand-Boutique mit ihrem Sortiment an hochwertigen Marken Einzigartigkeit. Damen werden sich über McQueen-Kleider und Chanel-Blazer zu Sonderpreisen freuen. Nebenan gibt's Männermode von YSL bis Watanabe und Shipley & Halmos, außerdem tolle Vintage-Shirts. Die Beratung, oft von den Besitzern selbst, ist aufmerksam, geschmackvoll und auf den Stil des Kunden abgestimmt. Hier findet man garantiert schnell genau das, was man sucht.

SHOPS

UNIONMADE

493 Sanchez Street // Castro
Tel.: +1 415 861 3373
www.unionmadegoods.com

Mon–Sat 11 am to 7 pm
Sun noon to 6 pm

K, L, M, S, T to Castro
F, J to Church / 18th
Bus 33 to 18th / Sanchez

Prices: $$$

MAP N° 41

If you get off the metro in Castro and stroll towards Valencia Street, you'll find plenty to discover. Ice cream shops, cafés, and designer boutiques like Unionmade, which, according to GQ, is "one of the best men's outfitters in the country." The store's signature concept, offering cool men's fashion at a fair price, has mass appeal. Handmade Alden shoes, leather jackets by Golden Bear, vintage working class outfits—a lot of the successful timeless selection is "made in America."

Steigt man an der Metro-Station in Castro aus und schlendert Richtung Valencia Street, gibt es jede Menge zu entdecken. Eisdielen, Frühstückscafés und Designerboutiquen wie das Unionmade, das laut GQ „einer der besten Herrenausstatter des Landes" ist. Das Konzept, die coolste Männermode zu fairen Preisen anzubieten, geht voll auf. Handgefertigte Alden-Schuhe, Lederjacken von Golden Bear, Arbeiterklamotten im Vintage-Stil – das Sortiment ist zeitlos und vieles davon „Made in America".

SHOPS

CARROTS

843 Montgomery Street
Financial District
Tel.: +1 415 834 9040
www.sfcarrots.com

Tue–Sat 11 am to 6 pm

F to The Embarcadero / Broadway
Bus 10, 12 to Pacific / Montgomery

Prices: $$$$

MAP N° 42

Carrots is a concept store for women. You'll find cashmere sweaters amidst perfume and exquisite vases. The racks are crowded with the newest fashion hot off the catwalks in Milano, Paris, or New York. All of this can be found in a picture perfect boutique that dazzles with chic interior design in a showroom of almost 4,000 sq. ft. Sisters Melissa and Catie Grimm want you to feel comfortable as you enjoy the finer things in life. The knowledgeable sales staff makes it all work.

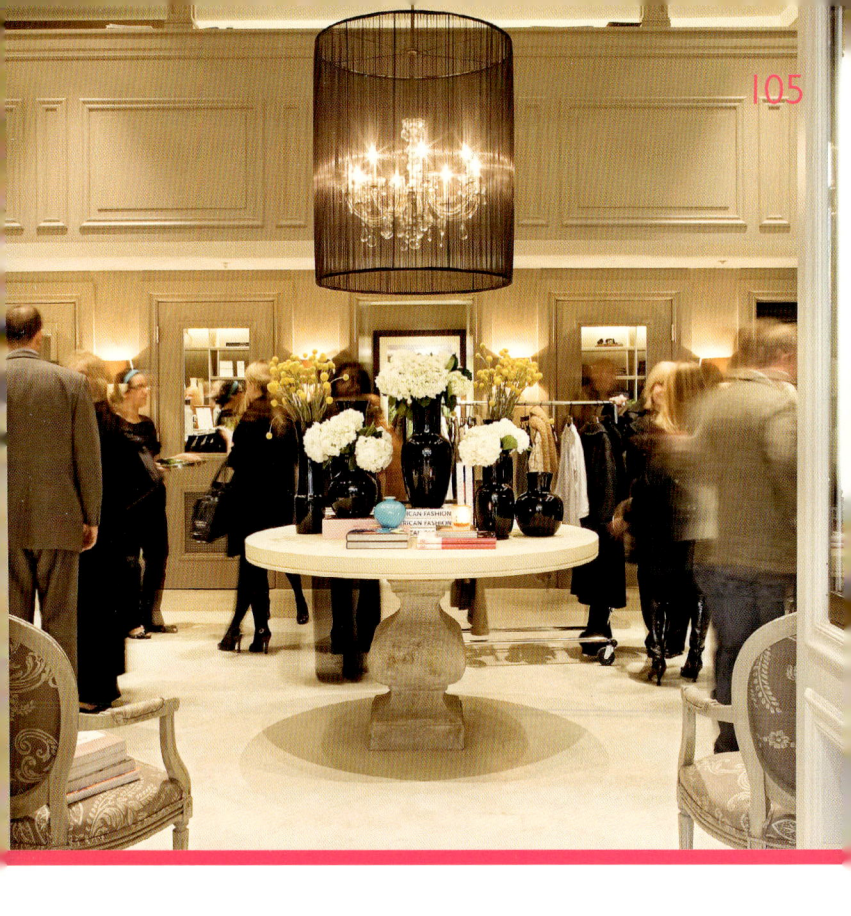

Das Carrots ist ein Concept Store für Frauen. Kaschmirpullis gibt es hier ebenso wie Parfüm oder edle Vasen. An den Kleiderständern hängt das Neueste von den Laufstegen in Mailand, Paris oder New York. Das Ganze in einer wahren Bilderbuchboutique mit mondäner Einrichtung und großzügigen 370 m² Fläche. Die beiden Schwestern Melissa und Catie Grimm wollen, dass man sich bei ihnen wohlfühlt und die schönen Dinge des Lebens genießt – das gelingt, auch dank des fachkundigen Personals.

SHOPS

AMOEBA MUSIC

1855 Haight Street // Haight-Ashbury
Tel.: +1 415 831 1200
www.amoeba.com

Mon–Sat 10.30 am to 10 pm
Sun 11 am to 9 pm

Bus 33, 66, 71, 71L to Haight / Stanyan

Prices: $$

MAP N° 43

For music collectors, this is the promised land: a retired bowling alley now crammed with over 100,000 albums, including an unrivaled selection of rare vinyl. Into underground '90s hip-hop? Math rock? Avant-garde Tokyo pop? It's all there – every genre is – plus booths for sampling. Surrender your ego and ask the famously knowledgeable staff for some recommendations, or just talk bands. An afternoon at Amoeba is a reminder that the pursuit of good music is a pursuit of love.

Das Gelobte Land für Musikliebhaber: eine alte Bowlingbahn, vollgestopft mit über 100 000 Alben, darunter eine einmalige Auswahl von seltenen Schallplatten. Hip-Hop der 90er gefällig? Oder Math-Rock und Avantgarde-Tokyo-Pop? Hier gibt's alles aus jedem Genre, inklusive Kabinen zum Reinhören. Lassen Sie ihr Ego vor der Tür und bitten Sie das fachkundige Personal um Tipps, oder tauschen Sie sich über ihre Lieblingsband aus. Im Amoeba weiß man: Die Liebe zur Musik ist wahre Liebe.

SHOPS

The clothes you'll find here are puritan and of the finest quality: sweaters, T-shirts, jeans—all from renowned labels like Alexander Wang, Allude, or Malene Birger, mixed and mingled with a few new discoveries. The interior decoration of the store follows the very same principle as the fashion: minimalist chic with straight lines. But what truly makes Dish special is the charming owner's expert advice, and her steady hand for elegant casual dress you want to keep all your life.

109

DISH

541 Hayes Street // Hayes Valley
Tel.: +1 415 252 5997
www.dishboutique.com

Mon–Sat 10 am to 7 pm
Sun noon to 6 pm

F to Market / Laguna
Bus 21 to Hayes / Laguna

Prices: $$$

MAP N° **44**

Die Kleidung, die man hier findet, ist puristisch und hat feinste Qualität: Pullover, T-Shirts, Jeans – alles von renommierten Labels wie Alexander Wang, Allude oder Malene Birger, dazu einige Neuentdeckungen. Die Einrichtung des Ladens folgt den Prinzipien seiner Mode: minimalistischer Schick mit geraden Linien. Was Dish so besonders macht, ist die Beratung der charmanten Eigentümerin und ihr Händchen für elegante Alltagsklamotten, die man sein Leben lang behalten möchte.

SHOPS

The scent of aroma oils, fresh cut flowers, and fresh fruit embraces guests of International Orange. Add to that jazz music and minimalistic design, because after all, the only thing that matters here is deep and lasting relaxation. The stressed body is supposed to activate its healing powers, no matter whether aided by yoga, massage, acupuncture, beauty treatments or the inevitable sunbathing session on the terrace. Gwyneth Paltrow and Julia Roberts swear by this recipe.

111

INTERNATIONAL ORANGE

2044 Fillmore Street, 2nd Floor
Lower Pacific Heights
Tel.: +1 415 563 5000
www.internationalorange.com

Mon–Fri 9 am to 9 pm
Sat–Sun 9 am to 8 pm

Bus 1BX to California / Fillmore
Bus 3, 22 to Fillmore / Pine

Prices: $$$

MAP N° 45

Der Duft von Aromaölen, Schnittblumen und frischem Obst umfängt die Gäste im International Orange. Dazu gibt es Jazzklänge und minimalistisches Design, denn hier dreht sich alles nur um eines: tiefe, anhaltende Entspannung. Der gestresste Körper soll seine Selbstheilungskräfte aktivieren, egal ob bei Yoga, Massagen, Akupunktur, Schönheitsbehandlungen oder dem anschließenden Sonnenbad auf der Terrasse. Gwyneth Paltrow und Julia Roberts sind große Fans von diesem Konzept.

SHOPS

Celia Sack is a real foodie. The sales floor of her small bookshop Omnivore (Latin: those eating food of both plant and animal origin) is stuffed with recent and antiquarian cookbooks, among them collectors' editions and historical tomes. You'll find titles like "Encyclopedia of Japanese Cuisine," or "Under the Walnut Tree," or "The Happy Glutton." If you are looking for inspiration and would rather read your recipes in a book than on your iPad, this is the store for you.

113

OMNIVORE BOOKS ON FOOD

3885 Cesar Chavez Street
(at Church Street) // Noe Valley
Tel.: +1 415 282 4712
www.omnivorebooks.com

Mon–Sat 11 am to 6 pm
Sun noon to 5 pm

BART 24th / Mission
F, J to Church / 27th

Prices: $$

MAP N° 46

Celia Sack liebt alles, was mit Essen zu tun hat. Die kleine Verkaufsfläche ihres Buchladens Omnivore (lat.: Allesfresser) ist vollgepackt mit neuesten und antiquarischen Kochbüchern, darunter Sammlerexemplare und wahre Geschichtswälzer. Sie tragen Titel wie „Die Enzyklopädie der japanischen Küche", „Unter dem Walnussbaum" oder „Der glückliche Vielfraß". Wer Inspiration sucht und seine Rezepte lieber vom Buch abliest statt vom iPad, kommt an diesem Laden nicht vorbei.

SHOPS

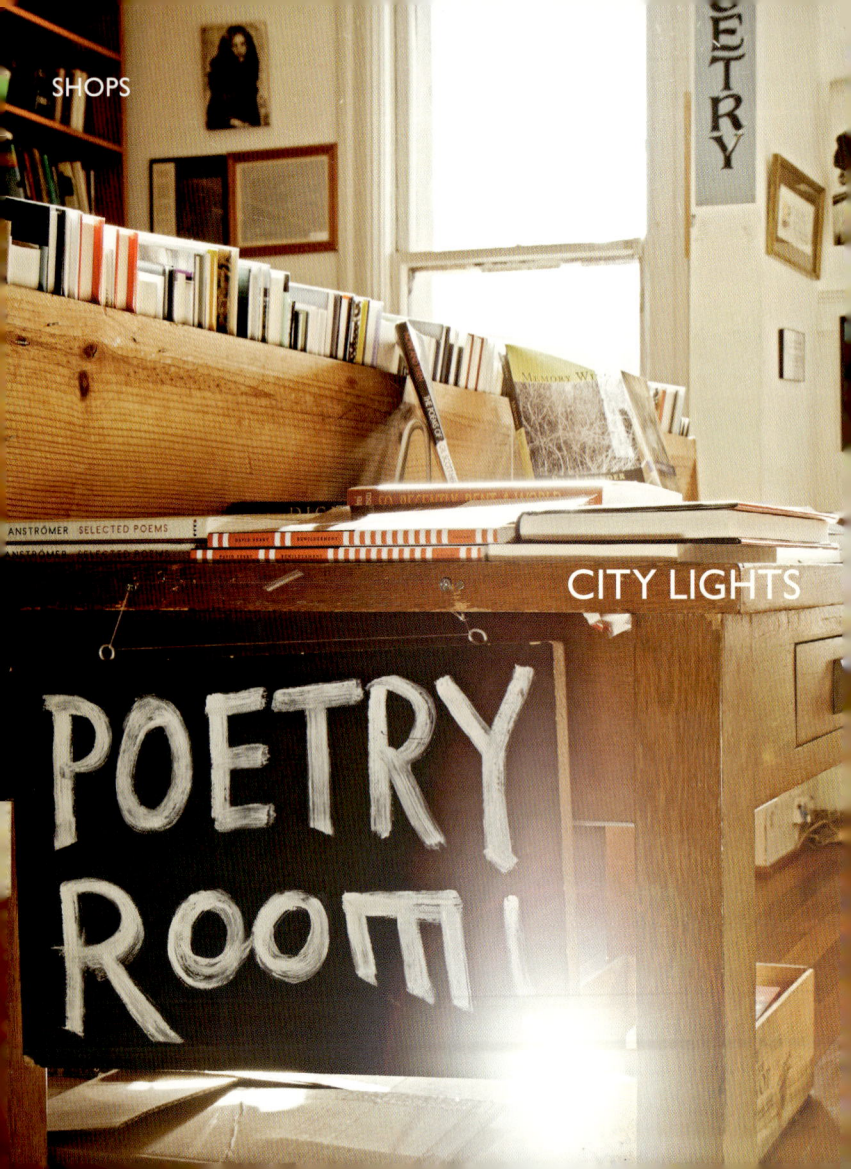

CITY LIGHTS

POETRY Room

115

SHOPS

CITY LIGHTS

261 Columbus Avenue // North Beach
Tel.: +1 415 362 8193
www.citylights.com

Daily 10 am to midnight

F to The Embarcadero / Broadway
Bus 8X, 8BX, 41 Columbus / Broadway
Bus 10, 12, 41 to Broadway / Grant

Prices: $$

The poets Ginsberg and Kerouac made it famous in the '50s, but City Lights is more than a "historic landmark"—it still earns its reputation as the radical indie bookstore everyone loves. The three-story maze of sunlit rooms is the ideal place to get lost for a few hours of browsing through sections like "Muckraking," "Dada," and "Balkan Fiction." The poetry floor alone is worth a pilgrimage; the frequent live readings still evoke the counterculture energy of the Beat founders.

Wegen der Autoren Ginsberg und Kerouac ist City Lights seit den 50ern berühmt-berüchtigt und wird dem eigenen Ruf als radikaler Indie-Buchladen noch heute gerecht. Im dreistöckigen Irrgarten sonnendurchfluteter Räume kann man sich ein paar Stunden lang zwischen den Regalen verlieren. Man findet Bücher über die Kunst des Skandals, Dada oder Belletristik aus dem Balkan. Allein die Etage für Poesie ist eine Reise wert. Regelmäßige Lesungen beschwören noch heute die Gegenkultur der Beat Generation.

MAP N° 47

SHOPS

PAUL'S HAT WORKS

6128 Geary Boulevard // Richmond
Tel.: +1 415 221 5332
www.hatworksbypaul.com

Tue–Sun 10 am to 6 pm

Bus 38, 38BX Geary / 22nd

Prices: $$$$

MAP N° **48**

Believe it or not, the "Four Pauls" are actually four charming young women, who bought this 1918 shop determined to breathe smart new life into neglected vintage fashion. Unabashedly anachronistic, they use antique tools (including "the conformateur," a steampunk fitting device) to handcraft bespoke hats in beaver, rabbit, or Montecristi straw for their most discerning customers (President Obama is one). A new hat "opens up possibilities," says one Paul. "You stand up taller."

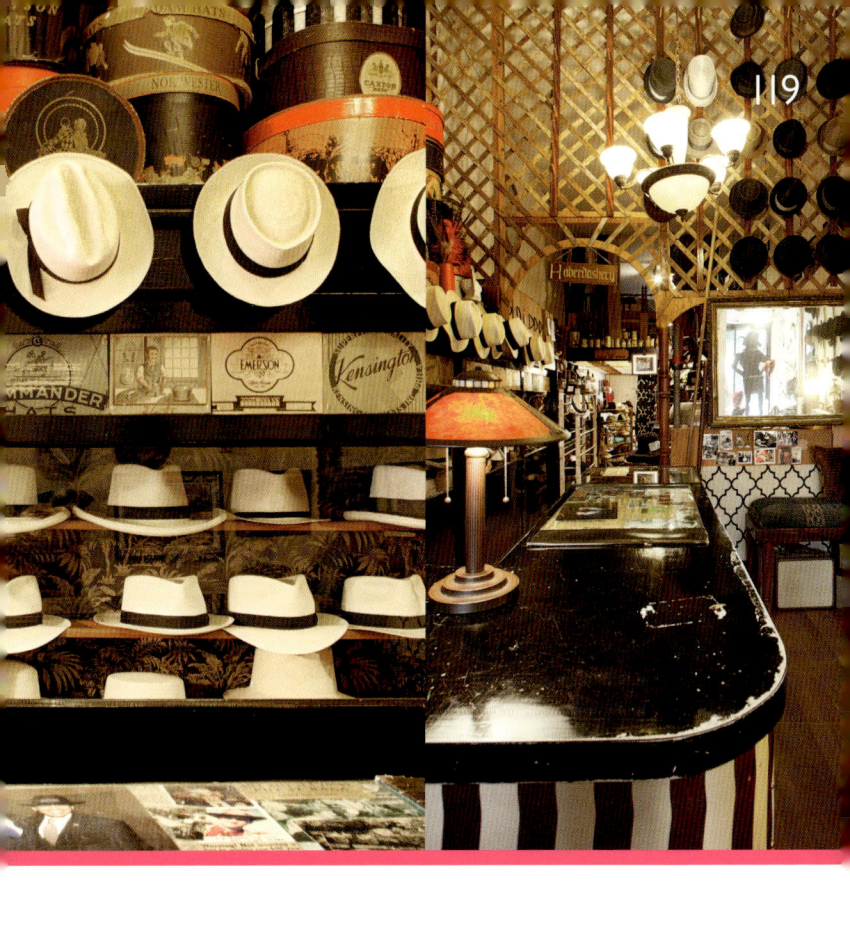

Hinter den „vier Pauls" stecken vier charmante junge Damen, die den Laden aus dem Jahr 1918 gekauft haben, um antiquierter Hutmode neues Leben einzuhauchen. Ganz anachronistisch benutzen sie antikes Werkzeug (wie etwa die Aufziehvorrichtung „Konformateur"), um maßgeschneiderte Kopfbedeckungen in Biber, Kaninchen oder Panamahüte herzustellen – Präsident Obama gehört zu ihren anspruchsvollen Kunden. „Ein neuer Hut erschließt neue Möglichkeiten", sagt ein Paul. „Er macht größer."

SHOPS

871 FINE ARTS

20 Hawthorne Street
South of Market (SoMA)
Tel.: +1 415 543 5812

Tue–Sat 10.30 am to 5.30 pm

BART, F, J, K, L, M, N, S, T
to Montgomery
Bus 30, 41, 45 to Howard /
New Montgomery

Prices: $$

MAP N° 49

Owner Adrienne Fish has an air of the shrewd librarian, and it's no wonder: For 26 years she has assembled the city's best collection of rare art books, and she's more knowledgeable about California artists than most museum curators. There's no better place to shop out-of-print titles, or just to admire and discuss the sketches, sculpture, and historical ephemera. 871 Fine Arts is a short walk from gallery row, and the art exhibits in the bookshop are reliably excellent.

Adrienne Fish hat etwas von einer schrulligen Bibliothekarin. Kein Wunder: Seit 26 Jahren sammelt sie seltene Kunstbücher. Sie besitzt die beste Kollektion der Stadt, und das dazu passende Kuratorenwissen über Künstler aus Kalifornien. Es gibt keine bessere Adresse für Raritäten oder für Gespräche über Skizzen, Skulpturen und historische Drucksachen. 871 Fine Arts liegt nur ein paar Schritte von der Galerien-Meile entfernt und zeigt verlässlich sehenswerte Kunstausstellungen.

SHOPS

THE VOYAGER SHOP

365 Valencia Street // The Mission
Tel.: +1 415 779 2712
www.thevoyagershop.com

Daily 11 am to 7 pm

F, J to Market / Church
Bus 14, 49 to Mission / 15th

Prices: $$$

MAP N° 50

The Voyager Shop houses several small stores under one roof. Their common denominator: All of them are well known and liked all around town. One of them is the surf shop Mollusk. The owners made their sales floor look like a submarine, with an interior design all in wood that conjures up images of the TV series "Lost." Particularly men will get their money's worth here. They can rummage through U.S. military sunglasses, magazines, leather accessories, and loads of cool clothes.

Mehrere kleine Geschäfte sind hier unter einem Dach vereint. Die Gemeinsamkeit: Alle haben sich in San Francisco bereits einen guten Namen gemacht, darunter der Surfshop Mollusk. Die Jungs haben ihre Verkaufsfläche in Form eines U-Bootes gebaut, aus Holz, mit einer Inneneinrichtung, die an die TV-Serie „Lost" erinnert. Vor allem Männer kommen im Voyager auf ihre Kosten und können neben US-Militär-Sonnenbrillen, Magazinen und Lederschmuck durch jede Menge cooler Klamotten stöbern.

CLUBS, LOUNGES +BARS

COOL
SAN FRANCISCO

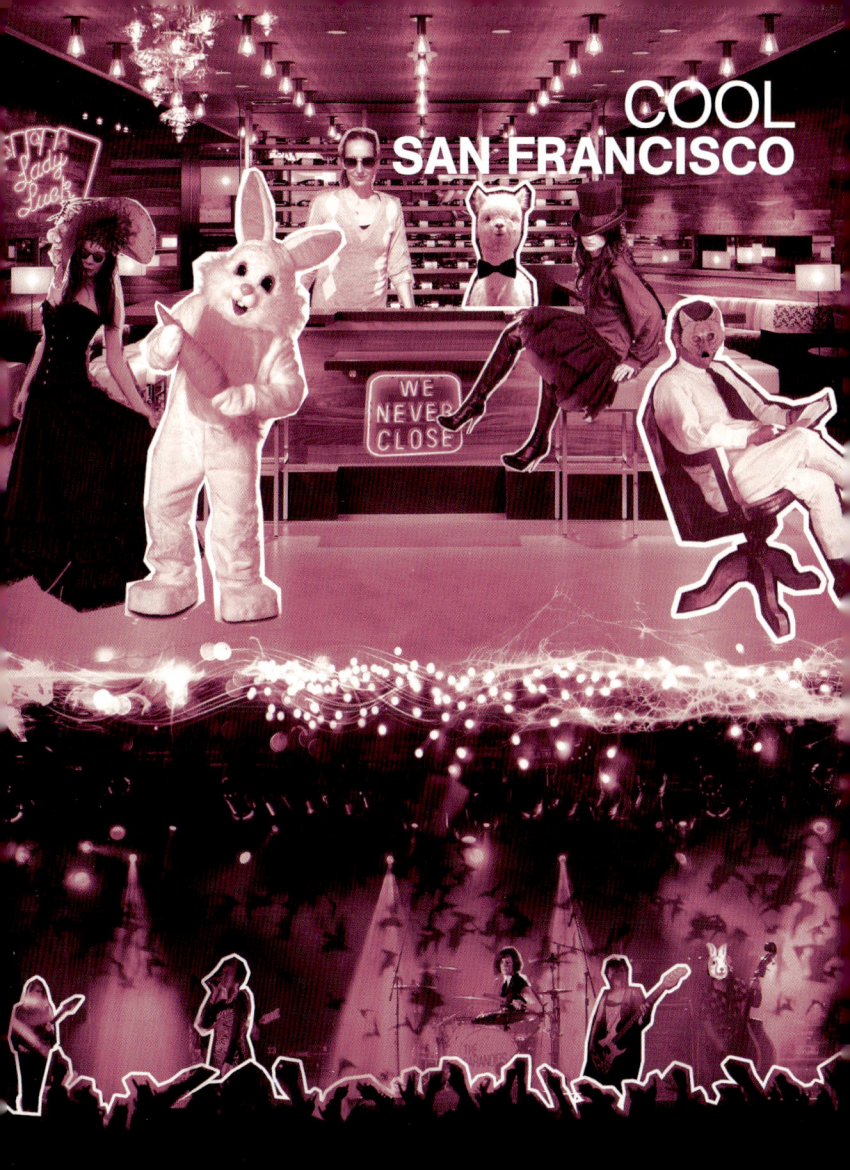

CLUBS,
LOUNGES
+BARS

The bartenders here are expert mixologists—try the rye, amaro, and ginger beer "In-Laws"—but the everyday whiskey sours are made with fresh juice, too. That's emblematic of Blackbird's relaxed but classy scene: The interior, papered with vintage disaster headlines, is artful without being pretentious; the crowd, a blend of straight and gay, is stylish but laid-back; the ambience is lively but (on weekdays) there are enough open couches to sit and enjoy some conversation.

BLACKBIRD

2124 Market Street // Castro
Tel.: +1 415 503 0630
www.blackbirdbar.com

Mon–Fri 3 pm to 2 am
Sat–Sun 2 pm to 2 am

F, J, K, L, M, S, T, Bus 22, 37, K-OWL, L-OWL, M-OWL to Church / Market

Prices: $$

MAP N° 51

Hinter der Bar stehen wahre Experten ihrer Zunft – „Inlaws", eine Mischung aus Whiskey, Amaro und Ingwerbier, beweist's. Ganz normalen Whiskey Sour mit frischem Saft gibt es aber auch. Überhaupt macht hier die Mischung das Flair aus: An die Wände sind alte Schlagzeilen gekleistert, die Einrichtung wirkt raffiniert ohne protzig zu sein. Die Kundschaft, homo und hetero, ist elegant aber locker. Unter der Woche bleibt genug Platz auf den Sofas, um sich in Ruhe zu unterhalten.

CLUBS,
LOUNGES
+BARS

LOCAL EDITION

691 Market Street // Financial District
Tel.: +1 415 795 1375
www.localeditionsf.com

Mon–Fri 5 pm to 2 am
Sat 7 pm to 2 am

BART to Montgomery
F, Bus 5, 6, 9, 9L, 21, 30, 31, 38, 38L, 45,
71, 71L, 800, K-OWL, L-OWL
to Market / Kearny

Prices: $$

MAP N° **52**

William Randolph Hearst once reigned over the world's most powerful newspaper empire. The basement where they once printed the "San Francisco Examiner," one of his papers, houses a bar today: the Local Edition. Surrounded by old press printing equipment, yellowed newspapers, and old-fashioned typewriters, elegantly dressed people gather for whiskey drinks at happy hour. Add to that old songs by Billie Holiday and Frank Sinatra, and you'll feel like a part of resurrected history.

William Randolph Hearst regierte einst das weltweit mächtigste Zeitungsimperium. In einem Keller, in dem der „San Francisco Examiner" gedruckt wurde, eine seiner Zeitungen, befindet sich heute eine Bar: die Local Edition. Zwischen altem Druckzubehör, vergilbten Zeitungen und antiquarischen Schreibmaschinen sitzen nun elegant gekleidete Menschen zur Happy Hour bei Whiskey-Drinks. Dazu laufen alte Songs von Billie Holiday und Frank Sinatra. Eine schöne Art, mit Geschichte umzugehen.

CLUBS,
LOUNGES
+BARS

BOTTOM OF
THE HILL

131

CLUBS, LOUNGES +BARS

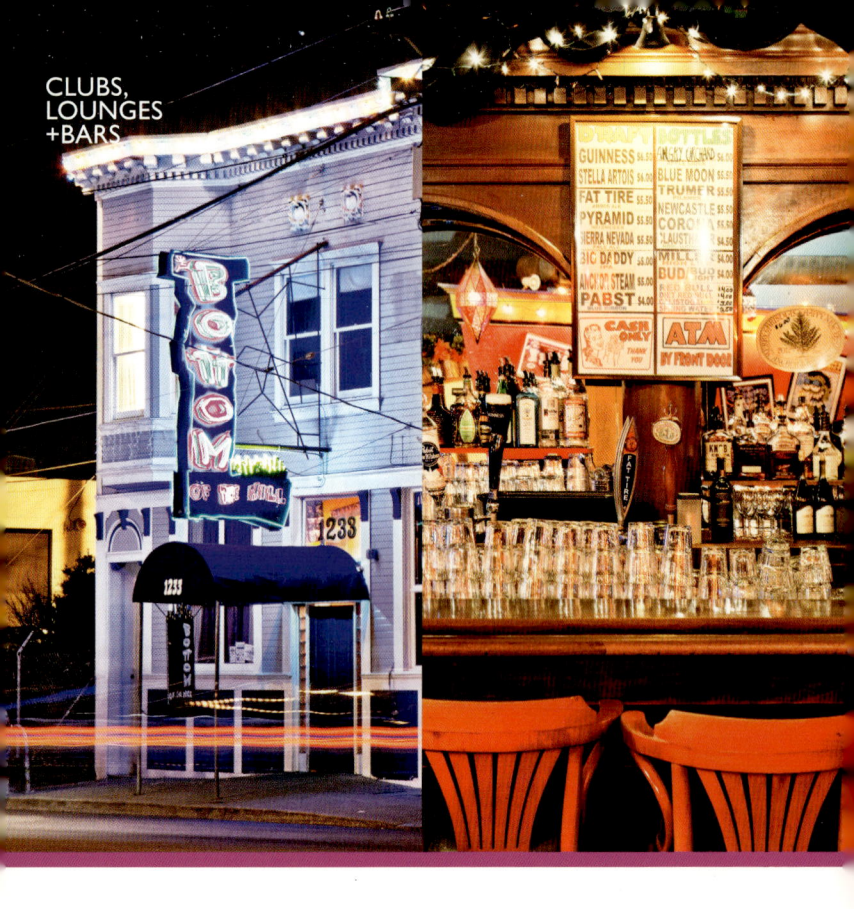

The old-west bar and funhouse-style main room are more odd than appealing, but nobody comes for the interior. They come because it's the city's best spot for punk, indie, country, and rock, six nights a week, in an intimate club where there are no bad seats in the house. Past "before-they-were-famous" acts include Marilyn Manson, the White Stripes, Green Day, Arcade Fire, and too many more to count. If the crowd gets too heavy, the outdoor patio is ideal for a smoke and some conversation.

BOTTOM OF THE HILL

1233 17th Street // Potrero Hill
Tel.: +1 415 626 4455
www.bottomofthehill.com

Daily 8.30 pm to 2 am

Bus 10, 22 to Connecticut / 17th

Prices: $

MAP N° 53

Die Bar wie aus dem Wilden Westen und eine Deko wie auf dem Jahrmarkt wirken zunächst etwas merkwürdig. Aber deshalb kommt man auch nicht her. Sondern weil es der heißeste Tipp für Punk, Indie, Country und Rock 'n' Roll ist – sechs Abende pro Woche. Viele Bands verdienten sich hier in intimer Club-Atmosphäre ihre Sporen: Marilyn Manson, The White Stripes, Green Day, Arcade Fire und viele mehr. Wenn es zu voll wird, bietet sich die Terrasse für eine Zigarettenpause und Unterhaltung an.

CLUBS,
LOUNGES
+BARS

PUBLIC WORKS

161 Erie Street // The Mission
Tel.: +1 415 932 0955
www.publicsf.com

Check website for details

BART to 16th / Mission
Bus 14, 49 to Mission / 14th

Prices: $$

MAP N° 54

Down a dirty alley in the Mission is an unexpectedly pleasant surprise: a vaulted warehouse where world-class DJs blast house, dubstep, and electronica until 4 am on weekends, with a Funktion One sound system and multiple bars to keep the hard-dancing, bohemian crowd happy. Meanwhile, the upstairs loft hosts more intimate live music, and the winding gallery shows works by artists in residence. Even better, they support non-profits: Part of the proceeds pay for art classes in local schools.

In einer dunklen Gasse im Mission District steht ein unscheinbares Warenhaus, in dem erstklassige DJs House, Dubstep und Electronica auflegen. Ein Funktion-One-Soundsystem und mehrere Bars machen die kunterbunte, hemmungslos tanzende Kundschaft bis 4 Uhr morgens glücklich. Oben geht's bei Livemusik familiärer zu, und an den Wänden hängen Werke regionaler Künstler. All das ist auch noch für einen guten Zweck: Ein Teil der Gewinne finanziert z. B. Kunstunterricht an San Franciscos Schulen.

CLUBS
LOUNGES
+BARS

ZEITGEIST

199 Valencia Street // The Mission
Tel.: +1 415 255 7505
www.zeitgeistsf.com

Daily 9 am to 2 am

F, Bus K-OWL, L-OWL, M-OWL,
N-OWL to Market / Buchanan

Prices: $

Visiting Zeitgeist is like dropping in on a biker neighbor's house party: The metal is heavy, the service is gruff, and the Bloody Marys are famously stiff. Yet the outdoor beer garden is a terrific microcosm of the entire city; hipsters, laborers, bankers, and bike nerds literally rub elbows at rough-hewn communal tables, drawn by big, cheap burgers and a sense of perpetual summer cookout. If the "Tamale Lady" shows up with her home-cooked Mexican delicacies, invest.

Im Zeitgeist geht's zu wie bei der Hausparty eines Bikers: dröhnender Heavy Metal, derber Service und berühmt-berüchtigte Bloody Marys. Der Biergarten ist ein Mikrokosmos der ganzen Stadt: Trendsetter, Arbeiter, Bankiers, Künstler und Fahrrad-Freaks tummeln sich wie bei einer Grillparty an langen Tischen, um die großen, aber billigen Hamburger zu genießen. Wenn die „Tamale Lady" auftaucht, sollte man unbedingt in ihre selbstgemachten mexikanischen Leckereien investieren!

MAP N° 55

HIGHLIGHTS

COOL
SAN FRANCISCO

HIGHLIGHTS

With its 1922 Spanish Baroque façade, sumptuous red velvet ceiling, and gold-leaf interior, the Castro is a throwback to a time when cinema symbolized class and charm. Live organ music precedes both classic and new-release movies, and sing-along nights to favorites like "The Sound of Music" and "West Side Story" come with party favors for patrons. Among the many annual film festivals are "Noir City," "Berlin and Beyond" (German), and, of course, "Frameline" (Gay and Lesbian).

141

THE CASTRO THEATRE

429 Castro Street // Castro
Tel.: +1 415 621 6120
www.castrotheatre.com

F, K, L, M, S, T to Castro
Bus 24, 35, 37, K-OWL, L-OWL, M-OWL to Market / Castro

Prices: $

MAP N° 56

Außen spanisches Barock der 1920er, innen Decken aus rotem Samt und vergoldete Wände. Das Castro beschwört eine Zeit, in der Kino Stil und Eleganz verkörperte. Ein Organist spielt live Musik, und bei Klassikern wie „The Sound of Music" und „West Side Story" singt das Publikum schon mal mit. Manchmal gibt's sogar filmgerechte Souvenirs. Und dann sind da noch die Filmfestspiele: „Noir City", „Berlin and Beyond" (auf Deutsch) und natürlich „Framelinc" (für die homosexuelle Szene).

HIGHLIGHTS ASIAN ART MUSEUM
MOON LEE CENTER FOR ASIAN ART AND C

In 2003, Italian architect Gae Aulenti pulled down interior walls from the city's old Beaux Arts library building to create this open, dramatic space for one of the largest collections of historic Asian art in the world, from Chinese calligraphy to Malay daggers to Persian miniatures. Yet the real highlight may be the frequent programs and performances, including Balinese concerts and Zen meditation lessons. The elegant, minimalist Japanese Tea Ceremony is highly recommended.

ASIAN ART MUSEUM

200 Larkin Street // Downtown
Tel.: +1 415 581 3500
www.asianart.org

Tue–Sun 10 am to 5 pm
Thu 10 am to 9 pm

Bus 5, 19 to Larkin / McAllister

Prices: $$

MAP N° 57

Die italienische Architektin Gae Aulenti riss 2003 die Innenwände der alten Stadtbibliothek nieder und schuf einen fast endlosen, dramatischen Raum für eine der weltweit größten Sammlungen asiatischer Kunst: Kalligrafie aus China, Dolche aus Malaysia, Miniaturen aus Persien und vieles mehr. Doch der wahre Höhepunkt des Museums sind die zahlreichen Veranstaltungen, wie etwa Konzerte aus Bali oder Zenmeditationen. Die elegante, minimalistische japanische Teezeremonie ist ein Geheimtipp.

HIGHLIGHTS

Its historicist architecture and granite façade match the city's older buildings, but the current library was opened in 1996, and its interior is a brilliant blend of traditional (lacewood and sycamore cabinetry) and modern (the steel-and-glass central atrium). Breathe deeply: The painted walls, glued floors, and carpets are built from non-gassing materials, so other than the dust from the books, the air is pure. The Gay & Lesbian Center has a dramatic trompe l'oeil ceiling.

SAN FRANCISCO MAIN LIBRARY

100 Larkin Street // Downtown
Tel.: +1 415 557 4400
www.sfpl.org

Mon, Sat 10 am to 6 pm
Tue–Thu 9 am to 8 pm
Fri noon to 6 pm
Sun noon to 5 pm

BART to Civic Center / UN Plaza
F, J, K, L, M, N, S, T to Civic Center
Bus 19 to Larkin / Grove

MAP N° 58

Die historizistische Architektur und Granitfassade passt zu den älteren Gebäuden der Stadt, doch die Bibliothek wurde erst 1996 eröffnet. Die Innenräume sind eine perfekte Mischung traditioneller (Regale aus Platanenholz) und moderner Elemente (Atrium aus Glas und Stahl). Tief durchatmen: Die gestrichenen Wände, Böden und Teppiche sind aus gasfreien Materialien, und außer Staub auf den Büchern ist die Luft rein. Das Gay & Lesbian Center hat eine beeindruckende Trompe-l'œil-Decke.

HIGHLIGHTS

Until the 1930s, the Ferry Building was the world's second busiest traffic junction, right after the Charing Cross Station in London. Today, one facelift later, the historical transfer hall with its arcades is the city's busiest market place. What's for sale here is palatable even to the most discerning gourmet, and those who cannot wait for their first bite can dig in right away at one of the tables in the hall. Enjoy ocean views at the open-air organic market three times a week.

FERRY BUILDING MARKETPLACE

One Ferry Building // Financial District
Tel.: +1 415 983 8030
www.ferrybuildingmarketplace.com

Mon–Fri 10 am to 6 pm
Sat 9 am to 6 pm
Sun 11 am to 5 pm

F to The Embarcadero / Ferry Building

Prices: $$$

MAP N° 59

Bis in die 30er Jahre war das Ferry Building, gleich nach der Charing Cross Station in London, der zweitgeschäftigste Verkehrsknotenpunkt der Welt. Nach einem Facelift ist die Abfertigungshalle mit ihren historischen Arkaden nun der lebendigste Marktplatz der Stadt. Hier wird alles verkauft, was gut riecht und schmeckt, mit Tischen für den ungeduldigen Gourmet, der nicht bis zu Hause warten will. Dreimal wöchentlich findet unter freiem Himmel ein Biomarkt mit Meerblick statt.

HIGHLIGHTS

During the California gold rush, thousands landed at these piers in pursuit of wealth, fortune, and happiness. Today, 150 years later, one of the city's most beautiful promenades spans right along the piers that extend far out into the picturesque bay. Pier 1, today offices for the Port of San Francisco, sits right next to the huge market halls. An architectural adventure from 1918, the building is made of steal and glass, and features a history wall that chronicles the life of the city and its port.

PIER 1

Pier 1 // Financial District
Tel.: +1 415 274 0488
www.sfport.com

Mon–Fri 8 am to 5 pm

F to The Embarcadero / Washington

MAP N° 60

Während des kalifornischen Goldrausches landeten hier Zehntausende auf der Suche nach Reichtum und Glück. Entlang unzähliger Piers, die sich weit in die malerische Bay hinausstrecken, findet sich heute, 150 Jahre später, eine der schönsten Flaniermeilen der Stadt. Gleich neben den riesigen Markthallen liegt Pier 1, ein architektonisches Abenteuer aus dem Jahr 1918, aus Stahl und Glas und mit einer History-Wall, die von der Geschichte der Stadt und ihres Hafens erzählt.

HIGHLIGHTS

CALIFORNIA ACADEMY OF SCIENCES

55 Music Concourse Drive
Golden Gate Park
Tel.: +1 415 379 8000
www.calacademy.org

Mon–Sat 9.30 am to 5 pm
Sun 11 am to 5 pm

Bus 44 to Concourse Drive
or Tea Garden Drive

Prices: $$

MAP N° 61

The California Academy of Sciences houses a rainforest with a living eco-system; and it houses the fascinating underwater world of the Amazon, including piranhas and anacondas. This natural history museum is alive inside and out, and, thanks to its glass structure, merges with Golden Gate Park. "It's like lifting up a piece of the park and putting a building under it," Renzo Piano explains his living roof structure which earned a Platinum LEED certification for sustainable architecture.

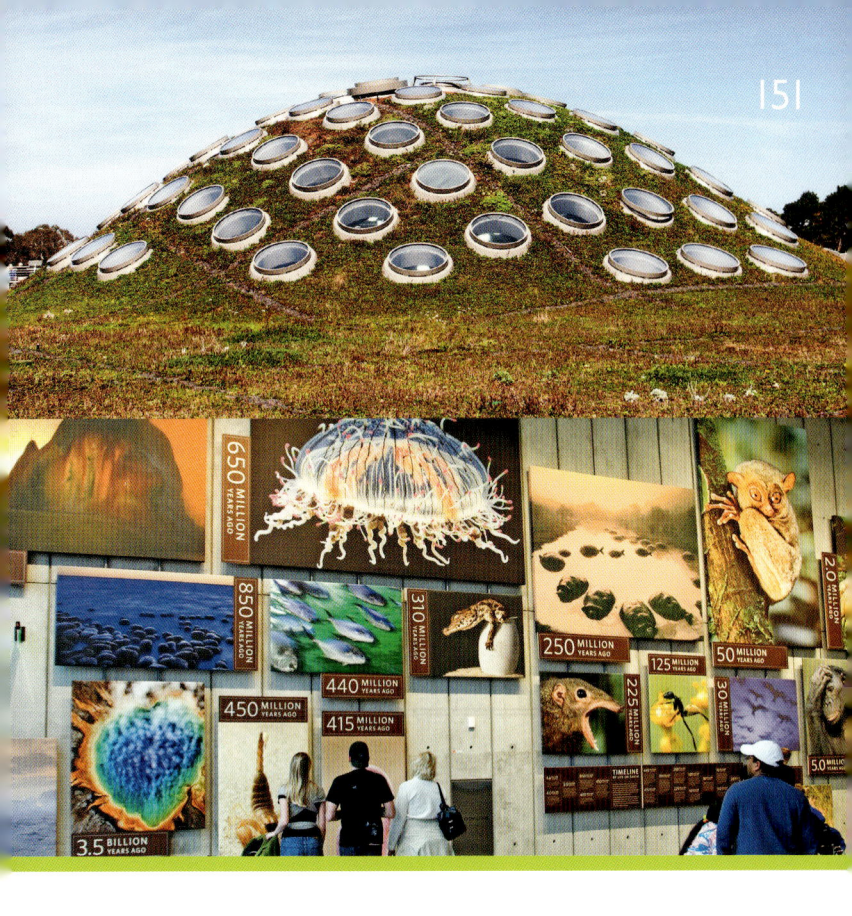

Hier findet sich ein ganzer Regenwald mit einem lebendigen Ökosystem. Oder die faszinierende Unterwasserwelt des Amazonas, Piranhas und Anakondas inklusive. Das Naturkundemuseum lebt innen und außen. Und verschmilzt dank seiner gläsernen Architektur mit dem Golden Gate Park. „Es ist, als hätte man einen Teil der Parkanlage hochgehoben und ein Gebäude darunter gebaut", erklärt Renzo Piano seine begrünte Dachkonstruktion, die eine Platin-Zertifizierung für umweltfreundliches Bauen erhielt.

HIGHLIGHTS

DE YOUNG
MUSEUM

153

HIGHLIGHTS

DE YOUNG MUSEUM 155

50 Hagiwara Tea Garden Drive
Golden Gate Park
Tel.: +1 415 750 3600
www.deyoung.famsf.org

Tue–Sun 9.30 am to 5.15 pm
Fri (March 29-November 29)
9.30 am to 8.45 pm

N to 9th / Irving
Bus 44 to O'Shaughnessy

Prices: $

The de Young Museum's observation tower juts above Golden Gate Park like the mast of a copper-clad ship in a sea of eucalyptus. Stowed below is a world-class permanent collection that ranges from American painters to African sculpture with surprising ease. Highlights include Cornelia Parker's "Anti-Mass," Ruth Asawa's wire abstracts, and Pop Art painter Wayne Thiebaud's "Three Machines." Often open late on Fridays for cocktails, live music, and artist demonstrations.

Der Aussichtsturm des de Young Museums ragt über dem Golden Gate Park wie der Mast eines Kupferschiffes in einem Meer von Eukalyptus-bäumen. Unten zeigt eine Sammlung von Weltklasse amerikanische Malerei bis afrikanische Skulpturen. Zu den Höhepunkten gehören Cornelia Parkers Skulptur „Anti-Mass", Ruth Asawas abstrakte Kabelkunst und die „Three Machines" von Pop-Art-Künstler Wayne Thiebaud. Freitags ist oft für Cocktails, Livemusik und Kunstvorstellungen länger geöffnet.

MAP N° 62

HIGHLIGHTS

BAKER BEACH

Battery Chamberlin Road // Richmond

Bus 29 Bowley / Gibson

It's not the Côte d'Azur, but on a summer day, Baker Beach does have a Mediterranean spirit: tipsy picnickers, dramatic cliffs, and even nude sunbathers (at the north end). When it's crowded, the beach feels like one big party; fitting, since it was the site of the original Burning Man festivals. Ironically, Baker Beach was once a military base—the historic "disappearing guns" are still mounted above the shore. Just north is a great hideaway cove, with occasional sea lions.

Zwar nicht die Côte d'Azur, aber am Baker Beach kommt an Sommertagen Mittelmeerstimmung auf: Picknicker, dramatische Felsen und nackte Sonnenanbeter (im nördlichen Teil). Wenn es voll wird, ist der Strand eine einzige Party. Das passt, denn hier fanden die ersten Burning Man Festivals statt. Baker Beach war einst ein Militärstützpunkt: Die „Verschwindlafetten" der Geschütze sind immer noch am Ufer montiert. Weiter im Norden gibt's eine versteckte Bucht, in der man ab und zu Seelöwen sieht.

HIGHLIGHTS

YERBA BUENA GARDENS

750 Howard Street
South of Market (SoMa)
Tel.: +1 415 820 3550
www.yerbabuenagardens.com

Daily 6 am to 10 pm

F, J, K, L, M, N, S, T to Montgomery
or Powell
Bus 8AX, 8BX, 8X, 30, 45, 91
to 3rd / Howard

MAP N° 64

Where else in San Francisco can one see stock brokers and the homeless sunbathing side by side? In 1999, this park won a national award for inclusiveness in urban design, and it truly has something for everyone: lawns, fountains, sculpture, a cinema, a bowling alley, and an ice rink. The restored 1906 carousel is fun, and a little haunting. There are seven museums, including SFMOMA, within two blocks of the gardens, so this is the place to lunch outdoors while museum hopping.

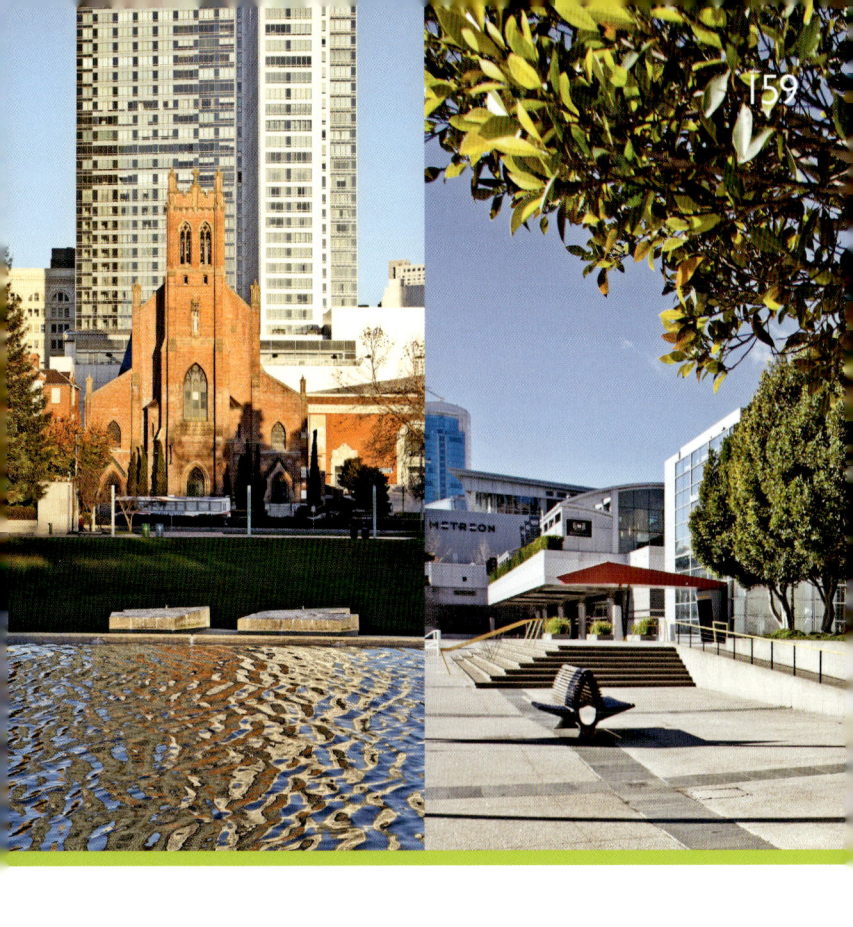

Nirgendwo sonst in San Francisco würden sich Börsenmakler neben Obdachlosen sonnen. 1999 gewann dieser Park einen Preis für soziale Inklusion in der Stadtplanung. Und tatsächlich gibt's hier für jeden etwas: Rasen, Brunnen, Skulpturen, ein Kino, eine Bowlingbahn und eine Eisbahn. Das restaurierte Karussell von 1906 ist toll, wenn auch ein bisschen gespenstisch. Wer eines der sieben Museen, darunter SFMOMA, im Umkreis von zwei Straßenzügen besucht, sollte im Park zu Mittag essen.

HIGHLIGHTS

GREAT AMERICAN MUSIC HALL

859 O'Farrell Street // Tenderloin
Tel.: +1 415 885 0750
www.gamh.com

Check website for details

BART to Civic Center / UN Plaza
F, J, K, L, M, N, S, T to Civic Center
Bus 19 to Larkin / O'Farrell

Prices: $$

With its columns, gold frescoes, and rococo balconies, the Great American Music Hall evokes a vintage opera house, which is appropriate, considering the high-quality bands that usually play this intimate stage. The building's history, however, is refreshingly dissolute: It was a renowned brothel during the city's famous "Barbary Coast" era. It's just as popular today—in fact, while the food is unremarkable, it's worth buying the "dinner ticket" to guarantee a seat during the show.

Die Säulen, goldenen Freskos und Rokoko-Balkons erinnern an ein uraltes Opernhaus. Das passt, denn auf der Bühne der Great American Music Hall spielen Bands von Weltklasse. Die Geschichte des Gebäudes ist allerdings erfrischend bunt: Als „Barbary Coast" noch das Rotlichtviertel der Stadt war, diente es als Bordell. Auch heute noch populär, lohnt es sich ein „Dinner-Ticket" zu kaufen, um einen sicheren Sitzplatz zu bekommen (auch wenn das Essen einen nicht vom Hocker haut).

HIGHLIGHTS

AREA 2881 GALLERY

2881 23rd Street (at Florida Street)
The Mission
Tel.: +1 415 648 9710
www.carlpisaturo.com

Sat 7 pm to 11 pm

BART to 24th / Mission
Bus 12, 48, 67 to 24th / Folsom
Bus 27 to Bryant / 23rd

Prices: $

MAP N° 66

This micro-museum is a scene from "Blade Runner," complete with undulating aircraft, swirling lights, and graceful robots. It's weird and whimsical, but it's also applied science. These are the designs of Carlo Pisaturo, a Stanford engineer who hand-builds kinetic sculptures to explore topics like "complex beam theory" or "multi-vector rotation." Thankfully, you don't need a technical degree to find his work compellingly strange and lovely. Call ahead for an appointment.

Ein Museum wie eine Szene aus „Blade Runner", mit schwebenden Flugobjekten, Lichtstrudeln und grazilen Robotern. Wirkt zwar etwas seltsam und skurril, ist aber angewandte Wissenschaft. Carlo Pisaturo, ein Ingenieur aus Stanford, stellt Skulpturen von Grund auf selbst her, um Themen wie „komplexe Strahlentheorie" und „Vektoren-Rotation" zu erforschen. Glücklicherweise braucht man kein technisches Studium, um seine Arbeit unwiderstehlich schön zu finden. Voranmeldung ist empfehlenswert.

HIGHLIGHTS

CLARION ALLEY

165

HIGHLIGHTS

Once an ugly slum, Clarion Alley now reflects the diversity and personality of the Mission itself, not just with Latin-American heritage art (though there are both Rivera-inspired walls and portraits of Kahlo), but also pro-labor paintings, graffiti-style logos, intellectual abstracts, flower power psychedelia, and leftist punk stencils. The Clarion Alley Mural Project replaces the paintings over time, making the alley itself a constantly evolving work of urban transformation.

167

CLARION ALLEY

Clarion Alley (between 17th and 18th, and Mission and Valencia)
The Mission

BART to 16th / Mission
Bus 14, 33, 49 to Mission / 18th

MAP N° 67

Einst war die Gegend ein hässliches Elendsviertel, heute ist die Clarion Alley Inbegriff der einzigartigen Vielfalt des Mission Districts. Lateinamerikanische Kunst (Kahlo-Porträts und Wandmalereien, die von Rivera inspiriert sind,) findet sich neben Arbeiterkunst, Graffitis, Konzeptkunst, psychedelischen Flower-Power-Bildern und linken Punkkritzeleien. Die Bilder werden immer wieder mit neuen Kunstwerken übermalt, sodass die Gasse ein Abbild des steten städtischen Wandels ist.

HIGHLIGHTS

This is where barbers work, not hairstylists. Sam Buffa, co-founder of F.S.C. Barber, insists on this distinction. Experts of the trade provide today's cutting edge at nine styling stations, equipped with mahogany framed mirrors and reminiscent of the good old days. An old record player doodles classic soul or jazz, while customers wait their turn on a wooden bench in the center of the room. By the way, female customers are welcome any time—if they can stomach a male cut.

F.S.C. BARBER

696 Valencia Street // The Mission
Tel.: +1 415 621 9000
www.fscbarber.com

Mon–Fri 9 am to 9 pm
Sat–Sun 9 am to 6 pm

BART to 16th / Mission
Bus 33 to 18th / Valencia

Prices: $$$

MAP N° 68

Hier arbeiten Barbiere, keine Friseure. Auf dieses Detail legt Sam Buffa, Mitbegründer von F.S.C. Barber, größten Wert. An neun Frisierstationen im Stil der guten alten Zeit, vor großen Spiegeln in Mahagonirahmen, folgen die Experten der Zunft den Trends von heute. Ein alter Plattenspieler dudelt klassischen Soul oder Jazz, während auf der Holzbank in der Mitte des Raumes die nächsten Kunden warten. Damen sind übrigens willkommen, sofern sie einen Herrenschnitt möchten.

HIGHLIGHTS

PHOTOBOOTH

171

HIGHLIGHTS

PHOTOBOOTH

1193 Valencia Street // The Mission
Tel.: +1 415 824 1248
www.photoboothsf.com

Wed–Sun 1 pm to 8 pm

BART to 24th / Mission
Bus 12, 48 to 24th / Valencia
Bus 14, 49 to Mission / 23rd

Prices: $$$

MAP N° 69

This tiny studio specializes in "vintage" portraits, but it's not 1970s retro, it's 1850s: the tintype. There's no film and no negative—just a single image in silver nitrate, exposed directly onto a metal plate. The results are beautiful, with deep, lustrous blacks and a particular liquid clarity, creating an intense, haunting portrait. Of course, you only get one shot, but owner Michael Shindler says, "that uncertainty is part of the excitement." Serious poses work best.

Dieses winzige Studio macht Porträts wie in guten alten Zeiten – aber nicht etwa wie in den 1950ern, sondern in den 1850ern. Ohne Film und Negative wird nur ein einziges Bild mit Silbernitrat direkt auf die Metallplatte belichtet. Satt schimmerndes Schwarz und fließende Transparenz schaffen ein tief beeindruckendes Porträt. Zwar hat man nur eine Chance, aber für Fotokünstler und Inhaber Michael Shindler ist gerade diese Ungewissheit Teil vom Erlebnis. Ernste Miene wirkt am besten.

HIGHLIGHTS

TWIN PEAKS

510-528 Twin Peaks Boulevard
Twin Peaks

Bus 36, 44, 48, 52
to Woodside / Portola

MAP N° 70

The wind is biting, but the view is worth it: a 360-degree sweep that takes in downtown, the South Bay, and the Golden Gate in one shot. Hiking the trails is the perfect way to appreciate the geography of San Francisco, or to marvel at the speed of the fog pouring in from the sea. After dark, Market Street burns like a cyberpunk artery, and the city lights pulse seductively—as is evidenced by the number of steamy car windows at the overlook. Yes, it's a good place for a date.

Trotz schneidendem Wind lohnt sich der Panoramablick auf Downtown, die South Bay und Golden Gate. Auf den Wanderwegen kann man die Geografie San Franciscos gut bewundern, oder staunen, wie schnell der Nebel vom Meer aufs Land zieht. Die Market Street glüht im Dunkeln wie eine Cyberpunk-Ader, und die Lichter der Stadt funkeln verführerisch. Beweis dafür sind die vielen beschlagenen Autofenster, die man hier sieht. Twin Peak ist ein perfektes Plätzchen für ein romantisches Rendezvous.

COOL DISTRICTS

THE MISSION / CASTRO / POTRERO HILL
The Mission is the city's most vibrant district—packed with cheap Latin food, colorful murals, mustached hipsters, and a bustling street, gallery, and party scene. Bordering Castro, America's largest gay neighborhood, has excellent boutiques, bars, and theaters. Social and political activism is integral to the area. Residential Potrero Hill also has some hip dive bars, Mexican food, and great city views from its usually sunny peak.

DOWNTOWN / UNION SQUARE / FINANCIAL DISTRICT / CHINATOWN / NORTH BEACH / SOMA / TENDERLOIN / LOWER PACIFIC HEIGHTS
Around Union Square, the world-famous shopping district, you'll find the diverse downtown districts: Financial District with modern high-rises and five-star hotels; the largest Chinatown outside Asia, featuring authentic food, colorful architecture, and import shops; North Beach, once the epicenter of beat culture, is now home to Little Italy's food; and South of Market (SoMa) ranges from the elite galleries of museum row to mixed nightclubs to warehouse slums. Tenderloin is the place to go for good live music and great dive bars while Lower Pacific Heights, called Upper Fillmore before gentrification, is a wealthy residential area, boasting shops and dining along Fillmore Street.

OUTER SUNSET / RICHMOND / MARINA / GOLDEN GATE PARK
Go to Outer Sunset for some cooling, near-constant wind at Ocean Beach, and afterwards, visit Richmond to warm your stomach with the amazing diversity of ethnic food (lots of Cantonese and Russian immigrants). Golden Gate Park to the south is the city's greatest public resource, home to numerous botanical gardens, two excellent museums, and frequent festivals. In Marina you'll find expensive but homogenous nightclubs, high-end shops on Union, and fine dining on Chestnut.

HAIGHT-ASHBURY
The hippie days are gone, but Haight Street still has an appealing variety of music stores, cheap ethnic food, secondhand shops, and local characters.

FISHERMAN'S WHARF
Long ago a trade center, it's now a tourist bazaar. Though, there are still fine views, good seafood, historic museums, and the boat to Alcatraz.

HAYES VALLEY
Sharp restaurants, interior design boutiques, trendy bars, high fashion, and up-and-coming art galleries suffuse this pocket neighborhood.

NOB HILL
Known for the sumptuous hotels surrounding Huntington Park, which features the lovely Grace Cathedral and a Romanesque central fountain.

NOE VALLEY
Popular with the bourgeois dot-com crowd, Noe Valley has a bustling sidewalk scene, primarily the cafés, bistros, and boutiques along 24th Street.

COOL MAP

PAGE | MAP N°

HOTELS

PAGE	MAP N°	
10	1	ADAGIO
12	2	CLIFT
14	3	FOUR SEASONS HOTEL SAN FRANCISCO
16	4	PHOENIX HOTEL
18	5	TAJ CAMPTON PLACE
20	6	HOTEL DES ARTS
24	7	HOTEL VITALE
26	8	ARGONAUT
28	9	HARBOR COURT HOTEL
32	10	THE HUNTINGTON HOTEL
34	11	HOTEL PALOMAR
36	12	THE MOSSER

RESTAURANTS +CAFÉS

40	13	ABSINTHE
42	14	FARALLON
44	15	FIFTH FLOOR
46	16	GITANE
48	17	ZUNI
50	18	GARY DANKO
52	19	BAR JULES
54	20	SUPPENKÜCHE
56	21	GREENS RESTAURANT
58	22	SWAN OYSTER DEPOT
60	23	CAFFE TRIESTE
62	24	OUTERLANDS
64	25	AZIZA
66	26	AQ
68	27	BAR AGRICOLE
70	28	SKOOL
72	29	SOMA STREAT FOOD PARK
74	30	ANDALU
76	31	CRAFTSMAN AND WOLVES
78	32	DELFINA
80	33	FLOUR + WATER
82	34	FOREIGN CINEMA
86	35	LIMON
90	36	LOCANDA
92	37	SLOW CLUB
94	38	NOPA
96	39	STATE BIRD PROVISIONS

SHOPS

100	40	SUI GENERIS
102	41	UNIONMADE
104	42	CARROTS
106	43	AMOEBA MUSIC
108	44	DISH
110	45	INTERNATIONAL ORANGE
112	46	OMNIVORE BOOKS ON FOOD
114	47	CITY LIGHTS
118	48	PAUL'S HAT WORKS
120	49	871 FINE ARTS
122	50	THE VOYAGER SHOP

CLUBS, LOUNGES, +BARS

126	51	BLACKBIRD
128	52	LOCAL EDITION
130	53	BOTTOM OF THE HILL
134	54	PUBLIC WORKS
136	55	ZEITGEIST

HIGHLIGHTS

140	56	THE CASTRO THEATRE
142	57	ASIAN ART MUSEUM
144	58	SAN FRANCISCO MAIN LIBRARY
146	59	FERRY BUILDING MARKETPLACE
148	60	PIER 1
150	61	CALIFORNIA ACADEMY OF SCIENCES
152	62	DE YOUNG MUSEUM
156	63	BAKER BEACH
158	64	YERBA BUENA GARDENS
160	65	GREAT AMERICAN MUSIC HALL
162	66	AREA 2881 GALLERY
164	67	CLARION ALLEY
168	68	F.S.C. BARBER
170	69	PHOTOBOOTH
174	70	TWIN PEAKS

178

COOL MAP

FISHERMAN'S WHARF
NORTH BEACH
COIT TOWER ON TELEGRAPH HILL
CHINA TOWN
TRANSAMERICA PYRAMID
WASHINGTON ST
FINANCIAL DISTRICT
FERRY BUILDING
EXPLORATORIUM
NOB HILL
UNION SQUARE
SOMA
TENDERLOIN
HAYES VALLEY
DOWNTOWN
THE MISSION
POTRERO HILL

EMERGENCY

Emergency number for Fire, Police, Ambulance: 911

ARRIVAL

BY PLANE

SAN FRANCISCO INTERNATIONAL AIRPORT (SFO)
13 miles / 21 km south of downtown San Francisco. National and international flights.

Free shuttle service AirTrain connects to the airport's rental car center and the Bay Area Rapid Transit station (BART) located in parking garage G.

BART ride from SFO to San Francisco costs about $8 one-way and runs frequently:
www.bart.gov
SFO is also connected to San Francisco by SamTrans routes 292, 397, and KX. Routes 292 and 397 are $2 to San Francisco, KX is $5. Large luggage is generally not permitted on the KX bus:
www.samtrans.com
A taxi from SFO to the city costs $40 and up each way, depending on traffic and the route (excluding the customary 15% tip). Cheaper, but longer: Shared vans will cost around $14 per person.

More airport information: **www.flysfo.com**

TOURIST INFORMATION

www.sanfrancisco.travel
SAN FRANCISCO'S VISITOR INFORMATION CENTER (VIC)
Tel.: +1 415 391 2000
900 Market Street
San Francisco, CA 94102
www.visitcalifornia.com/California-Welcome-Centers
Tel.: +1 415 981 1280
Pier 39 Concourse
San Francisco, CA 94133

ACCOMMODATION
www.booking.com/San-Francisco
hotels, bed & breakfast, rooms
www.craigslist.org/sfc
insider tip for finding short-term sublets
www.airbnb.com
privat rooms, apartment sharing
www.archstoneapartments.com
luxury apartments

TICKETS
www.tixbayarea.com
Tel.: +1 415 433 7827
tickets for San Francisco theater performances
www.citypass.com/san-francisco
pass gives free admission to main attractions
www.wharfpass.com
pass includes 10 attractions of Fisherman's Wharf, bay cruises, and sightseeing tours
www.ticketmaster.com
concerts, theater, culture, sporting events

COOL CITY INFO

www.stubhub.com
where fans buy and sell tickets for sports, theater, and concerts
www.goldstar.com
offers 50% off for theater, comedy, concerts, musicals, and sports
www.gotickets.com
sport, concert, and theater tickets

GETTING AROUND

PUBLIC TRANSPORTATION
www.sfmta.com
Municipal Railway (Muni) system runs a network of local transport, including cable cars, that covers most areas of touristic interest. MUNI consists of Muni Metro, busses (OWL = night bus), and the heritage streetcar F line (F Market & Wharves), which uses historic streetcars in original colors from several cities in the U.S. and Milan, Italy. MUNI also includes the world-famous cable cars, running on 3 lines in the steep streets between Market Street and Fisherman's Wharf.
www.bart.gov
Bay Area Rapid Transit (BART) is the regional metro and has 8 stations in San Francisco, making it a nice way to get between well-trafficked parts of the city, especially downtown and the Mission. Fares vary depending with distance traveled, and start at $1.75 for trips within the city. .
www.caltrain.com
Caltrain has 3 stops within San Francisco. It is useful for travel between San Francisco and communities on the Peninsula, Silicon Valley, or South Bay. Tickets must be purchased before boarding the train from ticket vending machines at any of the stations or from ticket clerks at staffed stations.

TAXI
Taxis are hard to find and hail, except for taxi stations at or near downtown business hotels or anywhere near Union Square. Calling for a cab can mean a 40-minute wait, if the cab shows up at all.

www.sfmta.com/cms/xcontact/ContactaTaxiCompany.htm
Taxi Commission's website showing a list of all licensed taxi operators.
www.yellowcabsf.com
Tel.: +1 415 333 3333
www.desotosf.com
Tel.: +1 415 970 1300
www.luxorcab.com
Tel.: +1 415 282 4141

BICYCLE RENTALS
San Francisco is fairly small in land area—just about 7 miles from north to south and 7 miles from east to west—but much of the terrain is very hilly and hard to pedal up. Do not be misled by maps depicting the city's street grid and assume these streets are always flat. SoMa, the Sunset, and Richmond districts are relatively flat.

www.sfbike.org
San Francisco Bike Coalition
Tel.: +1 415 431 2453
Keeps a lot of information about bike paths and bike routes on city streets. If you choose to ride a bicycle across the Golden Gate Bridge, be aware that walkers always stay on the east side of the bridge and bikes are often to ride on the west (ocean) side.
www.baycitybike.com
Tel.: +1 415 346 2453
www.bikeandroll.com
Tel.: +1 415 229 2000
www.blazingsaddles.com
Tel.: +1 415 202 8888
www.thebikehut.org
Tel.: +1 415 543 4335
www.pacbikes.com
Tel.: +1 415 928 8466

CAR RENTAL
www.budget.com
Tel.: +1 800 527 0700
www.alamo.com
Tel.: +1 877 222 9075
www.thrifty.com
Tel.: +1 888 400 8877
www.dollar.com
Tel.: +1 800 800 4000
www.rentawreck.com
Tel.: +1 415 282 6293
oldest and largest used car rental company
www.zipcar.com
Tel.: +1 866 494 7227
online membership car club service allows users to share cars by day or on hourly basis

CITY TOURS

www.sanfranciscosightseeing.com
Tel.: +1 888 428 6937
wide range of sightseeing tours by bus
www.sanfrancisco.ridetheducks.com
Tel.: +1 877 887 8225
fun vehicles travel the streets and the ocean
www.sanfranciscomovietours.com
Tel.: +1 800 979 3370
where movies and TV series have been shot

BOAT TOURS
Harbor tours guarantee marvelous views of the bay, the bridges, the island of Alcatraz and the city. Most tours leave at Fisherman's Wharf near Pier 39. Tickets can be purchased at kiosks along the waterfront walk.

www.hornblower.com
Tel.: +1 888 979 7152
brunch and dinner cruises
www.alcatrazislandtickets.com
Boat to Alcatraz departs from Pier 33. Buy Alcatraz tickets online, due to tickets selling out well in advance during busy months.
www.blueandgoldfleet.com
Tel.: +1 415 705 8200
serving Alameda, Angel Island, Oakland, Sausalito, Tiburon, and Vallejo
www.redandwhite.com
Tel.: +1 415 673 2900
bay cruises departing from Pier 43 1/2
www.goldengateferry.org
Tel.: +1 415 455 2000
a perfect way to travel from SF to Sausalito

COOL CITY INFO

FLIGHT TOURS
www.seaplane.com
Tel.: +1 415 332 4843
www.allsanfranciscotours.com
Tel.: +1 866 654 1410
www.sfhelicoptertours.com
Tel.: +1 800 400 2404

GUIDED TOURS
www.sftgg.org
Tel.: +1 415 753 8600
hire your personal tour guide
www.discoverwalks.com
Tel.: +1 415 494 9255
private tours by actual San Franciscans
www.precitaeyes.org
Tel.: +1 415 285 2287
mural art tour
www.architecturesf.com
Tel.: +1 415 264 8824
www.wokwiz.com
Tel.: +1 650 355 9657
Chinatown walking tours
www.gourmetwalks.com
Tel.: +1 855 503 0697
www.foottours.com
Tel.: +1 415 793 5378
fun game show/history walking tours
www.sfghosthunt.com
Tel.: +1 415 922 5590
www.haightashburytour.com
Tel.: +1 415 863 1621
Haight Ashbury Flower Power walking tour
www.cruisinthecastro.com
Tel.: +1 415 255 1821

ART & CULTURE

www.sfarts.org
monthly magazine for art and culture
www.sfgate.com/art
guide to the arts, museums, and galleries
www.theatermania.com/san-francisco-theater
guide to theaters, reviews, and ticket service
www.sfweekly.com/arts
news from museums, exhibits, and art related events

GOING OUT

www.metrowize.com
weekly publication dedicated to insider city and event info for SF
www.sfweekly.com
news, music, movies, restaurants, reviews, and events in SF
www.modernluxury.com/san-francisco
offers insightful coverage of national, regional, and local issues, as well as food, fashion, travel, and entertainment
www.timeout.com/san-francisco
guide to theater, restaurants, bars, movies, shopping, fashion, events, activities, music, art, clubs, tours, dance, and nightlife
www.blackboardeats.com
sign up to get insider perks (30% off your meal, free bottle of wine, exclusive prix fixes, etc.) at SF restaurants
www.fandango.com
movie tickets, movie times, trailers, reviews

COOL
CITY INFO

EVENTS

JANUARY TO MARCH

www.vietccsf.org
Celebrating New Year's Vietnamese style.
www.chineseparade.com
A colorful, vibrant parade with costumes, deafening firecrackers, martial arts groups, acrobats, and a 200-ft. Golden Dragon.
www.sresproductions.com/union_street_easter.html
The kid-friendly festivities include a petting zoo, pony rides, live music, train rides, alfresco dining, and a parade.

APRIL TO JUNE

www.nccbf.org
Cherry Blossom Festival. In Japantown, this kid-friendly event includes a parade, a street fair, and music.
www.haightashburystreetfair.org
People pack the Upper Haight for this event featuring local bands, food stalls, and plenty of shopping.
www.escapefromalcatraztriathlon.com
Participants (which often include world champions and Olympic medalists) swim 1.5 miles, bike 18 miles, and then run an extra 8 miles throughout the city.
www.sffs.org
San Francisco International Film Festival, showing art house movies, documentaries, and short films throughout the city.

www.unionstreetfestival.com
This festival attracts many local artists who display their arts and crafts, along with live jazz and classical music performances and an organic farmer's market.

JULY TO SEPTEMBER

www.visitfishermanswharf.com/fishermans-wharf/4th-of-july
Lots of free entertainment during the day, culminating with an impressive fireworks from the foot of Municipal Pier and from barges moored off the north of Pier 39.
www.sffringe.org
Fringe Festival is taking place at various theaters in the Civic Center/Tenderloin area. A 10-day festival about theatrical experimentation and having fun.

OCTOBER TO DECEMBER

www.sflovevolution.org
LovEvolution (formerly Love Parade and Love Fest) has become the largest public electronic music festival in the U.S.
www.sfblues.com
The oldest continually running blues fest in the world, attracting great blues performers.
www.sfcolumbusday.org/parade/index.html
A hugely popular parade celebrates Christopher Columbus and Italian heritage.
www.ghirardellisq.com/events/chocolate-festival/chocolate-festival
Theater, live music, and a 45-ft. Christmas tree decorated with ornaments, lights, and chocolate bars.

COOL CREDITS

Cover photo by Jo Weissgerber
Back cover photos: Spencer A. Brown, courtesy of Argonaut, Jeff Dow
Illustrations by Sophie Franke

pp. 2–3 (downtown view) by Martin Nicholas Kunz (further credited as mnk); pp. 6–7 (intro) by mnk

HOTELS

pp. 10–11 (Adagio) by Jeff Zaruba, 2009; pp. 12–13 (Clift) courtesy of Clift; pp. 14–15 (Four Seasons Hotel San Francisco) p. 14 top and 15 bottom by Gavin Jackson (further credited as gaja), others courtesy of Four Seasons Hotels & Resorts; pp. 16–17 (Phoenix Hotel) courtesy of Phoenix Hotel; pp. 18–19 (Taj Campton Place) courtesy of Taj Hotels; pp. 20–23 (Hotel des Arts) by gaja; pp. 24–25 (Hotel Vitale) by Cesar Rubio; pp. 26–27 (Argonaut) courtesy of Argonaut; pp. 28–31 (Harbor Court Hotel) p. 30 bottom by Markham Johnson, 2005, all courtesy of Harbor Court; pp. 32–33 (The Huntington Hotel) courtesy of Huntington Hotel SF; pp. 34–35 (Hotel Palomar) courtesy of Hotel Palomar; pp. 36–37 (The Mosser) by gaja

RESTAURANTS + CAFES

pp. 40–41 (Absinthe) by mnk; pp. 42–43 (Farallon) by mnk; pp. 44–45 (Fifth Floor) p. 44 top courtesy of Fifth Floor, others by mnk; pp. 46–47 (Gitane) by Jeff Dow; pp. 48–49 (Zuni) by mnk; pp. 50–51 (Gary Danko) by mnk; pp. 52–53 (Bar Jules) by Jo Weissgerber (further credited as jw); pp. 54–55 (Suppenküche) by mnk; pp. 56–57 (Greens Restaurant) by mnk; pp. 58–59 (Swan Oyster Depot) by mnk; pp. 60–61 (Caffe Trieste) by jw; pp. 62–63 (Outerlands) by mnk; pp. 64–65 (Aziza) by mnk; pp. 66–67 (AQ) by Spencer A. Brown; pp. 68–69 (Bar Agricole) by mnk; pp. 70–71 (Skool) p. 70 bottom courtesy of Skool, others by mnk; pp. 72–73 (Soma Street Food Park) by jw; pp. 74–75 (Andalu) p. 74 courtesy of Andalu, p. 75 by mnk; pp. 76–77 (Craftsman and Wolves) p. 76 by Aubrie Pick Photography, p. 77 by William Werner; pp. 78–79 (Delfina) by mnk; pp. 80–81 (Flour + Water) by Eric Wolfinger; pp. 82–85 (Foreign Cinema) by mnk; pp. 86–87 (Limon) courtesy of Limon; pp. 90–91 (Locanda) by Eric Wolfinger; pp. 92–93 (Slow Club) by mnk; pp. 94–95 (Nopa) courtesy of Nopa; pp. 96–97 (State Bird Provisions) by Freda Banks

SHOPS

pp. 100–101 (Sui Generis) courtesy of Sui Generis; pp. 102–103 (Unionmade) courtesy of Unionmade; pp. 104–105 (Carrots) by Drew Altizer; pp. 106–107 (Amoeba Music) p. 106 by Jay Blakesberg, p. 107 courtesy of Amoeba Music; pp. 108–109 (Dish) courtesy of Dish; pp. 110–111 (International Orange) courtesy of International Orange; pp. 112–113 (Omnivore Books on Food) p. 113 top courtesy of Omnivore Books on Food, others by jw; pp. 114–117 (City Lights) by jw; pp. 118–119 (Paul's Hat Works) by mnk; pp. 120–121 (871 Fine Arts) by mnk; pp. 122–123 (The Voyager Shop) by mnk

CLUBS, LOUNGES + BARS

pp. 126–127 (Blackbird) by mnk; pp. 128–129 (Local Edition) by mnk; pp. 130–133 (Bottom of the Hill) by mnk; pp. 134–135 (Public Works) courtesy of Public Works; pp. 136–137 (Zeitgeist) p. 136 left (2) courtesy of Zeitgeist, others by jw

HIGHLIGHTS

pp. 140–141 (The Castro Theatre) by Steven Underhill; pp. 142–143 (Asian Art Museum) courtesy of Asian Art Museum; pp. 144–145 (San Francisco Main Library) p. 145 top by Richard Barnes, others by Tim Hursley; pp. 146–147 (Ferry Building Marketplace) p. 146 by David Wakely/www.david-wakely.com, others by Richard Barnes; pp. 148–149 (Pier 1) by Richard Barnes; pp. 150–151 (California Academy of Sciences) courtesy of California Academy of Sciences; pp. 152–155 (de Young Museum) pp. 152–153 by Rafael Ramirez Lee/Shutterstock, p. 154 left top by mnk, others by Mark Darley; pp. 156–157 (Baker Beach) by mnk; pp. 158–159 (Yerba Buena Gardens) p. 158 top courtesy of Yerba Buena Gardens, others by mnk; pp. 160–161 (Great American Music Hall) p. 160 top by Chris Oldaker, other courtesy of Great American Music Hall; pp. 162–163 (Area 2881 Gallery) p. 163 bottom courtesy of Area 2881 Gallery, others by mnk; pp. 164–167 (Clarion Alley) by mnk; pp. 168–169 (F.S.C. Barber) by Ingalls Photo; pp. 170–173 (Photobooth) by 2010 Jonathan F.; pp. 174–175 (Twin Peaks) by luxora/shutterstock, p. 175 by mnk; p. 190 (Pier 39) by Petra Schwarzwald

pp. 178–179 (map) courtesy of www.openstreetmap.org/copyright/en

COOLCITIES
POCKET GUIDES

COOLCITIES NEW YORK

WITH SPECIAL TIPS FROM VALESCA GUERRAND HERMES

teNeues

A NEW GENERATION
of multimedia lifestyle travel guides featuring the hippest, most fashionable hotels, shops, dining spots, galleries, and more for cosmopolitan travelers.

- BARCELONA
- SAN FRANCISCO
- VIENNA
- PARIS
- MUNICH
- NEW YORK
- AMSTERDAM
- HAMBURG
- LONDON
- ROME
- MILAN
- FRANKFURT
- BERLIN

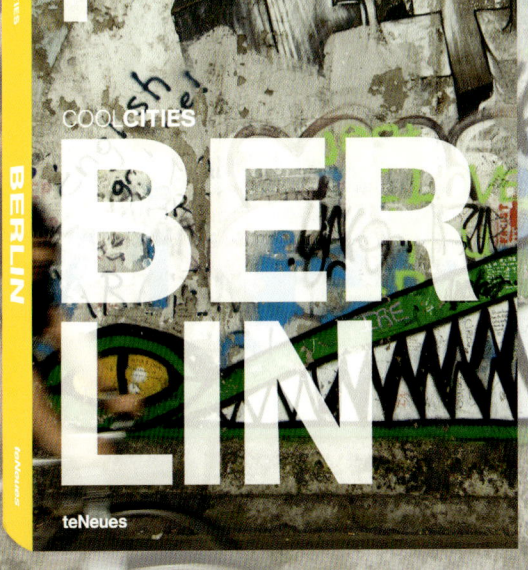

www.cool-cities.com

COOLCITIES
APPS for iPhone/iPad/iPod Touch

APP FEATURES

Search by categories, districts, or geolocator;
get directions or create your own tour.

VISUAL

Discover the city with tons of
brilliant photos and videos.

© 2011–2013 Idea & concept by Martin Nicholas Kunz, Lizzy Courage Berlin
Selected and edited by Martin Nicholas Kunz, Josia Lamberto-Egan, Sabine Wabnitz, Jo Weissgerber
Introduction and location texts by Josia Lamberto-Egan, Sabine Wabnitz
Editorial Management: Regine Freyberg
Editorial Assistance: Julia Preuß
Photo Editor: David Burghardt
Copy Editor: Dr. Simone Bischoff
Layout and pre-press: Sophie Franke
Imaging: Andreas Doria, Hamburg
Translations: Dr. Helga Schier

© 2011–2013 teNeues Verlag GmbH + Co. KG, Kempen

teNeues Verlag GmbH + Co. KG
Am Selder 37, 47906 Kempen // Germany
Phone: +49 (0)2152 916-0, Fax: +49 (0)2152 916-111
e-mail: books@teneues.de

Press department: Andrea Rehn
Phone: +49 (0)2152 916-202 // e-mail: arehn@teneues.de

teNeues Digital Media GmbH
Kohlfurter Straße 41–43, 10999 Berlin // Germany
Phone: +49 (0)30700 77 65-0

teNeues Publishing Company
7 West 18th Street, New York, NY 10011 // USA
Phone: +1 212 627 9090, Fax: +1 212 627 9511

teNeues Publishing UK Ltd.
12 Ferndene Road, London SE24 0AQ, UK
Phone: +44 (0)20 3542 8997

teNeues France S.A.R.L.
39, rue des Billets, 18250 Henrichemont // France
Phone: +33 (0)2 4826 9348, Fax: +33 (0)1 7072 3482

www.teneues.com

Picture and text rights reserved for all countries. No part of this publication
may be reproduced in any manner whatsoever. All rights reserved.

While we strive for utmost precision in every detail, we cannot be held
responsible for any inaccuracies, nor for any subsequent loss or damage arising.

Bibliographic information published by the Deutsche Nationalbibliothek.
The Deutsche Nationalbibliothek lists this publication in the
Deutsche Nationalbibliografie; detailed bibliographic data are
available in the Internet at http://dnb.d-nb.de.

Printed in the Czech Republic
ISBN: 978-3-8327-9706-5

COOLCITIES SAN FRANCISCO METRO MAP